Julius Caesar's Disease

I dedicate this book to my parents Carla and Stefano and to the dearest memory of my grandparents Rina and Bruno.

Francesco M Galassi

To my beloved wife Leanne and my dear parents Susan and Jamshid.

Hutan Ashrafian

Julius Caesar's Disease

A New Diagnosis

Francesco Maria Galassi
and Hutan Ashrafian

PEN & SWORD
HISTORY

First published in Great Britain in 2016 by
Pen & Sword History
an imprint of
Pen & Sword Books Ltd
47 Church Street
Barnsley
South Yorkshire
S70 2AS

ISBN 978 1 47387 078 9

A CIP catalogue record for this book is available from the British
Library

Typeset in Ehrhardt by
Mac Style Ltd, Bridlington, East Yorkshire
Printed and bound in the UK by CPI Group (UK) Ltd,
Croydon, CR0 4YY

Pen & Sword Books Ltd incorporates the imprints of Pen & Sword
Archaeology, Atlas, Aviation, Battleground, Discovery, Family
History, History, Maritime, Military, Naval, Politics, Railways, Select,
Transport, True Crime, Fiction, Frontline Books, Leo Cooper,
Praetorian Press, Seaforth Publishing and Wharncliffe.

For a complete list of Pen & Sword titles please contact
PEN & SWORD BOOKS LIMITED
47 Church Street, Barnsley, South Yorkshire, S70 2AS, England
E-mail: enquiries@pen-and-sword.co.uk
Website: www.pen-and-sword.co.uk

Contents

Acknowledgements

The authors wish to express their gratitude to all the academics, historians and physicians, whose precious help, observations, critique and suggestions have enriched this research. In particular, words of gratitude go to Imperial College London and the Unit of Surgery and Cancer for having allowed the development of research projects about ancient history analytics in the light of modern medicine; to Professor Paul A Cartledge (A G Leventis Professor of Greek Culture Emeritus, Clare College, The University of Cambridge) for his authoritative insights into the psychology and historical details of Julius Caesar's emulation of Alexander, as well as for his interest and curiosity for this new theory involving both historical and clinical knowledge; to Professor Christopher B R Pelling (former Regius Professor of Greek at Christ Church College, Oxford University) for his very helpful and powerful commentary on the subtleties of the Plutarchean text; to Professor Robert C T Parker (Wykeham Professor of Ancient History, New College, Oxford University) for his very interesting clarification of the social role of epilepsy in the ancient world; to Professor Federico Maria Muccioli (University of Bologna) for a very interesting conversation on the reasons for the survival of the epileptic theory throughout history. The authors also wish to thank Professor Barry S Strauss (Chair of the History Department at Cornell University) and Professor Carl W Bazil (Chief of the Division of Epilepsy and Sleep at Columbia University) for fruitfully sharing their personal views – which, like our own, combine both medicine and studies of the classics – on Caesar's health, as well as Professor Kristina Killgrove (Department of Anthropology, University of West Florida) for commenting on the theory and for giving their views the prestigious space offered by her successful bioarcheology feature in *Forbes Magazine*. Kind thanks also to Dr Jessica Hughes (The Open University) for covering the authors' research and allowing them to explain it at length in visual form in one of her interviews for the brilliant UK YouTube channel *Classics Confidential*, and to Professor Trevor Luke (Department of Classics, Florida State University) for giving them his insightful feedback on Caesar's last days and his aspiration to being a divine ruler.

Moreover, Francesco M Galassi wishes to thank Professor Frank J Rühli, Dr Thomas Böni and the whole Institute of Evolutionary Medicine (University of Zurich) for allowing him to continue and expand his research scope incorporating the research method and approaches first developed at Bologna and at Imperial College. He also thanks his colleagues Michael Habicht (IEM Zurich) for his precious historical advice and Dr Raffaella Bianucci (Department of Legal Medicine, University of Turin) for her invaluable suggestions on Caesar's malaria. He also thanks Dr David L Smith (Selwyn College, The University of Cambridge) for constant and enlightened support of his historical researches, Emeritus Professor Alessandro Ruggeri (DIBINEM, University of Bologna) for his powerful mentorship when he was a student and for his support of the theory, as well as the anthropologist Professor Giorgio Gruppioni (University of Bologna, Ravenna Campus) for his genuine interest in the 'philologico–clinical' method and for offering his personal feedback on the theory. For their interest and support of a further development of the study on Caesar, Francesco Galassi wishes to thank Professor Giovanni Giorgini (Department of Political and Social Sciences, University of Bologna), as well as Mr Lorenzo Gasperoni and Mr Leonardo Belli for liaising to promote classical education in the Romagna area. Last, but far from being the least, special thanks go to his boyhood friend Lorenzo Lazzarini (Ancient Philosophy PhD student at the University of Saint Andrews) for spending long hours analytically dissecting the historical likelihood of epilepsy in Caesar's case and critically discussing its potential political and historical relevance and for his kind support of his literary efforts.

For his part, Hutan Ashrafian wishes to thank Professor Stephen Chan (School of Oriental & African Studies) for their whimsical discussions of history and politics, Professor Lord Ara Darzi (Imperial College London) for his continued encouragement in the pursuit of excellence and Professor Thanos Athanasiou (Imperial College London) for enthusiasm and innovative brilliance.

Finally, the two authors wish to say thank you to all the friends, colleagues, distant and close, who have supported this historico-medical study from its first steps and the publication of the research letter in *Neurological Sciences* in March 2015. Their words and inputs have played a tremendous role in their decision to persevere with this project and they will never forget their positive influence.

Francesco M Galassi & Hutan Ashrafian

Preface

Why Caesar's Health Matters and the Need for a Philologico-Clinical Approach

'Take we the course which the signs of the gods and the false dealing of our foes point out. The die is cast.'[1] It was with the utterance of this fatal sentence that on 11 January 49 BC the Roman proconsul C Julius Caesar marched armed against the Roman Republic, crossing the border represented by the river Rubicon and defying orders to dismiss his legions and subdue himself to senatorial authority. After five years of campaigns in Gaul, Britain and Germany, the time had come for this victorious and insatiable commander to accomplish what even the most audacious and popular strategists of Rome (namely Scipio the Elder, Marius, Sulla and Pompey) had never been able to attain: the definitive transformation of an old oligarchic state into a monocratic Mediterranean superpower. Whether Caesar succeeded in achieving this goal or not may still be open to debate within the historical community, yet it is undeniable that his lightning attack on the Italian peninsula, quick submission of Pompeian Spain and incredible capacity to resist and endure incumbent defeat in Greece, ultimately culminated in his complete victory at Pharsalus in 48 BC which opened to him the doors of absolute domination. This success allowed him to seize control of the Roman state imposing his dictatorial yoke on what had not yet been vanquished of the *vetus ordo*. Animated by towering ambition and the 'sacred' mission to bring his family and himself back to the honours and prestige that being of direct descent from Venus herself should guarantee, he led his almost invincible soldiers to nearly every corner of the Roman world, crushing his enemies, external and internal, one by one, until the final bloody victory over Pompey's sons at Munda, in Spain, in 45 BC. His name was soon to become associated with power itself and would for centuries onwards be synonymous with imperial authority.[2]

Not long before fulfilling, according to some sources, his dream to invade the Parthian Empire, following in the footsteps of Alexander the Great, he lost his last battle, this time unarmed in that traditionally weapon-free place which was the Senate House at the hands of a handful of conspirators who had deluded themselves into thinking that, through the tyrant's *excidium*, the then long-dead and corrupt *res publica* could be born again. While his earthly path had come to an abrupt end, his imperial design was taken up by his followers (Mark Antony and Octavian) who extirpated the threat represented by Caesar's murderers at Philippi in 42 BC. Octavian's ultimate victory over Antony and his lover Cleopatra meant the establishment of a more Italo-centric, *primus-inter-pares*-styled princedom. Julius Caesar, the most notable exponent and hero of the *gens Iulia* was elevated to the rank of god and a cult of *Divus Iulius* was established in Rome, conferring upon him the aura and sacrality of myth.

The poet John Dryden once famously wrote, 'All things are subject to decay,/And when fate summons, monarchs must obey.'[3] While Caesar may well be regarded as an invincible military leader, he was by no means invulnerable and like every human being he suffered from physical and psychological ailments. Throughout the centuries he has been handed down to us as affected by epilepsy, a condition that allegedly caused him to fall and suffer from fits even, in the words of Suetonius, *inter res gerendas* (in stately affairs). Such accounts met with widespread success and soon grew popular with the general public, inspiring later reinterpretations and novels: how would it be possible to forget the beautiful and powerful images of the suffering old hero created by William Shakespeare's pen? Virtually nobody has ever questioned this assumption and most of the research has focused on the possible etiologies of Caesar's epilepsy. Nevertheless, when the original Greco-Roman sources are re-examined, many a clinical and philological doubt arises about the real nature of Caesar's conditions suggesting the following epistemological questions:

a. Can one be absolutely sure that *morbus comitialis* always meant epilepsy? In particular, in Caesar's case for which one has but so few and little informative descriptions in the ancient sources, how is it possible to endorse the epileptic theory without first questioning its foundations?

b. Caesar's ancestors and close successors' ailments have been used to construct familial trees of epilepsy, but have his relatives' symptoms been interpreted correctly?

c. In terms of clinical rationale and odds, how likely would it have been for him to suffer from some other condition than epilepsy?

d. Had he – or his successor Octavian – realised that the debilitating condition he suffered from was, to quote the German philosopher Nietzsche '*Menschliches, Allzumenschliches*', 'human, all too human', to fit his heroic public profile, would it not have been more convenient, in a propaganda drive, to support the idea that he might have been affected by a neurological condition (ie epilepsy) which had gripped prominent protagonists of ancient history, was associated with genius and was – in spite of the curse it may represent at a superficial reading – sent by the gods?

e. How devastating was Caesar's medical condition and what role did it play in his final years and months of power? To what extent can one attempt to determine if it had any part in the timing of his demise and final political decisions?

This book, the natural follow-up investigation to a recently published neurological article[4] on the topic of the real nature of the Roman leader's ailments, shall endeavour to answer these questions, offering new insights and new angles from which to look at the same long-debated subject.

Discussing health conditions and illnesses of famous characters from a bygone age may indeed be considered a daunting prospect and the advantages stemming from it could be questioned.

Our answer to this is that disease and medicine do play and have always played a role in human affairs, often determining the course of history or at least influencing the natural progression and resolution at crucial junctures of the past. Laurel-wreathed and on marble pedestals as our imagination may wish them to stand, historical characters are yet still humans exposed to physical decay, injuries and the laws of genetics. A carefully rigorous analysis of the ancient sources allows researchers to formulate new hypotheses in the light of current medical discoveries and this all adds fundamental knowledge to the foundations of historical research. Though political decisions or tactical moves ought to be analysed and attributed the eminent value they obviously deserve, health conditions ought not to be consigned to footnotes, nor should observations on them be regarded as ancillary knowledge to be produced in a spirit of reverence and submission to received – and little investigated – theories. Having it clear in mind that it is no easy task to formulate thoroughly exact medical diagnoses after so many centuries from the discussed events, a cautious and sound mixture of philological analysis and most advanced and contextualised diagnostic principles will be the guiding spirit of this study. The evidence, the assumptions, the reported accounts and even the gossip collected in the ancient sources will be dissected and their likelihood will be discussed in depth, to understand to what degree we can trust them and how informative and truthful allies of a frank and large scale reassessment of Caesar's health they can be found to be.

In the dedication of his masterpiece *The Prince* Nicolò Machiavelli, highlighting the necessity of different perspectives when in the act of judging an object and, to some extent in a very farsighted anticipation of microscopic powers of magnification and reduction, most famously wrote: 'For those who draw maps place themselves on low ground, in order to understand the character of mountains and other high points, and climb higher in order to understand the character of the plains. Likewise, one needs to be a ruler to understand properly the character of the people, and to be a man of the people to understand properly the character of rulers.'[5] Taken out of their political context, such powerful words brilliantly depict the authors' attitude when tackling this enigmatic paragraph of a most eventful chapter of Roman history.

By respectfully dissociating themselves from the stances and approaches of the historians and medical researchers who studied this issue merely showing interest for the pathophysiology and etiology of an *a priori* accepted disease, we shall try to look into the complex puzzle of Caesar's health conditions from a distance, going back to the very primordial conundrum: Was Caesar really epileptic? What is the evidence for it?

We tackle this question by means of a novel methodology. Integrating practical hands-on clinical experience within our perspective of cutting-edge contemporary biomedical science we appraised the historical sources of Caesar. Our background in the philology of Latin and Greek meant that studying ancient sources offered a uniquely integrative view of Caesar's life and pathology. This led to a new diagnosis. The following pages will look into his symptoms and his behaviour in his final years, critically examining all theories and interpretations so far proposed, highlighting their likelihood as well as exposing their weaknesses. Through this we aim to offer a comprehensive explanation for Julius Caesar's final dark mood and decline, at the very moment that the Roman Empire underwent its own birth by an allegorical caesarean section.[6]

Chapter One

The Ancient Sources and the Birth of the Epileptic Theory

Ever since his rise to power rivers of ink have been used to describe the military and political endeavours of Julius Caesar to the extent that even the most minute aspects of his life, including gossip, plots, love affairs, can be easily reconstructed by historians. It is indeed no surprise that they still account for verbose passages and voluminous chapters even in contemporary biographies of the Roman dictator. When it comes to his health, however, very limited information can be retrieved from the historical accounts. To the great regret of historians, clinicians, bioarchaeologists and paleopathologists, it is no longer possible to seek data in his mortal remains, as, for instance, has been the case in recent years for the bony remains found in Vergina (Macedonia, northern Greece) generally attributed to Philip II of Macedon (382 – 366 BC).[1] According to tradition, Caesar's body was burned during his public and highly emotional funeral in Rome, as was the Roman custom. As the biographer Suetonius reports:

'When the funeral was announced, a pyre was erected in the Campus Martius near the tomb of Julia, and on the rostra a gilded shrine was placed, made after the model of the temple of Venus Genetrix; within was a couch of ivory with coverlets of purple and gold, and at its head a pillar hung with the robe in which he was slain. Since it was clear that the day would not be long enough for those who offered gifts, they were directed to bring them to the Campus by whatsoever streets of the city they wished, regardless of any order of precedence. At the funeral games, to rouse pity and indignation at his death, these words from the "Contest for the Arms" of Pacuvius were sung:—

"Saved I these men that they might murder me?"

and words of like purport from the "Electra" of Atilius. Instead of a eulogy the consul Antonius caused a herald to recite the decree of the Senate in which it had voted Caesar all divine and human honours at once, and likewise the oath with which they had all pledged themselves to watch over his personal safety; to which he added a very few words of his own. The bier on the rostra was carried down into the Forum by magistrates and ex-magistrates; and while some were urging that it be burned in the temple of Jupiter on the Capitol, and others in the Hall of Pompey, on a sudden two beings with swords by their sides and brandishing a pair of darts set fire to it with blazing torches, and at once the throng of bystanders heaped upon it dry branches, the judgment seats with the benches, and whatever else could serve as an offering. Then the musicians and actors tore off their robes, which they had taken from the equipment of his triumphs and put on for the occasion, rent them to bits and threw them into the flames, and the veterans of the legions the arms with which they had adorned themselves for the funeral; many of the women too, offered up the jewels which they wore and the amulets and robes of their children."[2]

Thus the prospect of finding parts of his famed body are virtually non-existent. Incredible and unlikely as it may sound to the ears of archaeologists, despite the several centuries that divide us from its last sighting, the discovery of the body of Alexander the Great (356–323 BC) would still be a more likely eventuality, given that no direct mention of its destruction is found in the available literary sources. In Caesar's case this would be judged as absolutely beyond the realm of reason by any serious researcher. This undeniable shortcoming sadly means that no measures of the proportions of his body may be taken, no facial reconstruction based on the frontal surface of the osseous scaffold of his skull will ever be possible, nor clear signs of battle-caused wounds, of congenital or acquired deformities could possibly be identified through a rigorous gross anatomical examination. Likewise, no information about his diet and behaviour could be retrieved from an osteological analysis and no genetic nor biochemical state-of-the-art tests capable of solving, or at least furnishing more hard evidence on, the riddle of his health conditions will be ever performed. Similarly, in spite of a few scholarly commendable

– yet very limited in their outcomes – attempts to identify cachexia or even pathologically meaningful cranial deformity respectively in numismatic and sculptural effigies of the Roman general are unlikely to provide any decisive information on his alleged and potential pathologies since their styles and looks are quite varied and one can merely hope to attain a blurred perception of what Caesar might really have looked like. With respect to this, at best we can catch a glimpse of his appearance through the so called Tusculum head, now in Turin, which was probably made when Caesar was still alive.[3] Along with other sculptural representations, whose attribution is often uncertain, it gives what Professor Christopher Pelling most exactly defined an 'overall impression of a high brow, thinning hair, deep-set eyes, a large curved nose, hollow cheeks, a pointed chin, and a long, thin, often creased neck with a prominent Adam's apple.'[4]

From a passage in Appian's second book of the Civil Wars we collect further relevant information:

'While they were in this temper and were already near to violence, somebody raised above the bier **an image of Caesar himself made of wax. The body itself**, as it lay on its back on the couch, **could not be seen.** The image was turned round and round by a mechanical device, **showing the twenty-three wounds in all parts of the body and on the face** that had been dealt to him so brutally. The people could no longer bear the pitiful sight presented to them.'[5]

This is the proof that at least one waxen image – such images portraying men of rank were usual in Roman funerals – of Caesar's face existed: obviously, unlike marbles and minted coins which are but the artist's interpretation, this would be the representation closest to Caesar's real lineaments. Marble and metal have survived for two thousand years but unfortunately that did not make it to our age for us to behold and study. Another reference of this kind to an image of himself Caesar held in his house is found in the account of the day of his assassination by Dio Cassius which interprets it in an ominous sense, at the same time describing Caesar's scepticism for such 'divine' admonitions at that point of his life:[6]

'Therefore they sent Decimus Brutus, as one supposed to be his devoted friend, to secure his attendance. This man made light of Caesar's scruples and by stating that the senate desired exceedingly to see him, persuaded him to proceed. At this **an image of him**, which he had set up in the vestibule, **fell of its own accord and was shattered in pieces**. But, since it was fated that he should die at that time, he not only paid no attention to this but would not even listen to someone who was offering him information of the plot.'[7]

It is really a hard task to determine whether also this image was waxen or a marble one since Dio Cassius uses the word εἰκών τις αὐτοῦ [*eikón tis autoû*, 'an image of him'] which very generally compared to Appian's much more precise word choice: 'ἀνδρείκελον αὐτοῦ Καίσαρος ἐκ κηροῦ πεποιημένον' [*andreíkelon autoû ek keroû pepoieménon*, 'a man-portraying image of Caesar himself made of wax'].

In any case, both would have helped understanding his real facial traits since they were made when he was still alive.

Such being the case, it comes as no surprise that most specialised discussions on Caesar's physical and psychological sufferings actually identify their reason for being in a handful of densely and deeply reckoned sentences penned several decades after Caesar's life, namely the biographies by the already mentioned authors Suetonius (c 69–after 122 AD) and Plutarch of Chaeronaea (c 46–127 AD). Although further, or parallel, information is also found in other ancient authors, such as Dio Cassius (c AD 155–235), Titus Livius, Velleius Paterculus (c 19 BC–c. AD 31), Appian (c AD 95–c. AD 165), Nicolaus of Damascus (first century BC) from whom we will draw later in our analysis, those two *Lives of Caesar* still nowadays represent the first resource for anyone interested in catching an authoritative overall glimpse of Julius Caesar's life, from the beginning to its tragically abrupt conclusion. These historical accounts, composed in the second century AD, represent the product of a complex moulding of material dating back to Caesar's day, in which different traditions, including both pro-Caesar sources and anti-Caesar ones, contributed to the genesis of deep and insightful accounts which would shape our perception of Caesar for many centuries. It is through them that philologists and historians endeavour to reconstruct the original sources, written by authors who were close to Caesar and part of his life as a statesman and military commander, thus supposedly based upon first hand vital evidence, now long lost.[8]

At this stage one should ask himself how to treat Caesar's own literary production, mainly his *Commentarii*, the accounts of his military campaigns in Gaul, Germany and Britain (*De Bello Gallico, On the Gallic War*), against his civil adversaries (*De Bello Civili, On the Civil War*), as well as three other writings, *Bellum Alexandrinum* (*The Alexandrian War*), *Bellum Africum* (*The African War*) and *Bellum Hispaniense* (*The Spanish War*), whose author most certainly is not Caesar himself, but some deputy of his, who could directly draw from the general's correspondence, dispatches and war plans. Those accounts, defined as 'free of all oratorical adornment as a naked body free of clothing' by Caesar's political opponent and master of oratory Marcus Tullius Cicero (106–43 BC), are of little use when assessing his health, since they merely focus on the military and political events and clearly serve the propaganda goal of extolling their author and protagonist's deeds to the Roman public opinion. It is therefore futile to look for decisive medical information on his health in those documents, while they may still be useful when reassessing the military context in which episodes of illness are reported to have occurred.

Having now deployed a full array of available sources and methodologies that will be used in this research and having acknowledged the inevitable limitations imposed by lack of first-hand or bioarchaeological material, the purpose of this first chapter will be to minutely list and arrange all relevant medical and biological information on Julius Caesar in chronological order, following his life as narrated by the sources. At the end of this initial section, the readers will clearly see how history could not help but decree Caesar an epileptic, a diagnosis which we will dissect, revisit, and question and respectfully – both towards tradition and towards the learned colleagues who opted or may still opt for it – overturn in following chapters. We shall start from his birth, pathological information about his family members, his youth, physical and psychological traits, eventually to cover the more famous episodes of his purported 'falling sickness'. From now on, however, there will be nothing but the facts, in the best Julian and, at the same time, clinical tradition accompanied by a robust commentary to help our readers understand them better and make up their own minds about them.[10]

Classical scholars tend to agree on 13 July 100 BC as the date on which Julius Caesar was born although historically there has been some debate on whether 101 or 102 BC should not be taken as more exact dates as, had he been born in 100 BC, he would not have been old enough to hold certain magistracies.[11] This position seems to have been strongly advocated by Theodor Mommsen (1817–1903), the famous German historian, who maintained that, if that date be accepted, then Caesar would have entered all of his offices before the legal age. An interesting counterargument is furnished by Napoleon III (1808–1873), an admirer and biographer of Julius Caesar, who underlined how 'this objection, certainly of some force, is dispelled by other historical testimony. Besides we know that at Rome they did not always observe the laws when dealing with eminent men.'[12] From a medical perspective, one or two years more or less do not represent a major point and one can be fairly sure that when Caesar died (44 BC) he was aged 56 or, if those other proposed dates are accepted, then 57 or 58, thus slightly more of a middle-aged man for our times, a man approaching old age, if not already well into it, by Roman standards.[13]

He was born into the *gens Iulia*, a patrician family once glorious and respected who boasted to descend, via Iulus and his father Aeneas, from the love-goddess Venus. The hard truth was in fact that the family was far from its apogee since they could not afford any more respectful mansion than a modest house in the Suburra, an infamous neighbourhood of Rome located on the slopes of the hills *Viminalis* and *Quirinalis*, an overpopulated residential area inhabited mostly by the vulgar, which still evokes images of crime, profanity and indecency. Such a sharp contradiction, somewhat undesirable for any person of ambition, especially for one who would soon start dreaming of world domination and *sui generis* emulation of Alexander the Great, may from the very start have shaped his psychology. Hence it is sensible to look at the very maternal stage onto which he made his first appearance as the prefiguration of his more mature unquenchable thirst for glory, conquest and ruthless removal of anyone who stood between him and his objectives.

He was the son of C Julius Caesar (c 130 BC–85 BC), who had been questor, praetor and proconsul of Asia, and of Aurelia Cotta (120 BC–54 BC). According to the historian Pliny the Elder (c 23 AD–79 AD) Caius Julius Caesar senior died in Pisa when his son was only 16 years old. This was a sudden and unexplainable death: one morning, as he was putting on his shoes, he collapsed. The verb 'collapse', used by Adrian Goldsworthy to describe this episode, is probably the most accurate translation made so far since it captures the meaning of the Latin '*exanimatus est*', which conveys the notion of being deprived of breath at once, thus of suddenly passing away extremely weakened.[14] More specifically, in the same passage Plinius talks about two Caesars, the identity of the second being generally thought to be Lucius Julius Caesar (*praetor urbanus* in 166 BC), namely the protagonist of this book's great grandfather. He seems to have passed away while on duty in a similar fashion to his grandson (ie the dictator's father). As we will have opportunity to examine later in detail, these two sudden deaths – largely ignored or underestimated by research – may play a prominent, if not vital, role in understanding Julius Caesar's disease.[15]

Aurelia on the other hand enjoyed a longer life and, like the famous Cornelia (c 189–110 BC), mother of the Gracchi, won her place in the pantheon of notable Romans as the ideal matron. Again following the description provided by Napoleon III – clearly mirroring comments by Tacitus (c 56 AD –after 117 AD) and Plutarch – she appears to have been 'a woman of lofty character and severe morals' who 'helped above all in the development of his great abilities, by a wise and enlightened education, and prepared him to make himself worthy of the part destiny had reserved for him'.[16] This is undoubtedly a pompous statement, yet its essential truth ought to be added to the aforementioned early psychological imprints and inputs he received, which would shape his character. These signs, strong and largely unseen in ordinary men as they are, are natural and can be easily traced throughout Caesar's life. They should never be attributed to neurological or psychiatric diseases, unless one wishes to reinterpret history too freely and risk being largely in the wrong. If one really wants to 'patho-biologise' Caesar's character and psychology – that is, attributing his behaviour to a certain disease he might have had – one may then at best, as we shall see, work out and weigh with a pinch of salt the influence played by disease on those very natural psychological features. Moreover, when assessing such influence, it is important to focus on the last segment of Caesar's life, avoiding unsubstantiated psychopathological speculation on his early years.

We have said that Aurelia lived a long life. Indeed, this is of seminal importance to discard a wrongly long-held misconception which associates the very name Caesar with the term *caesarean birth*.[17] It has even been believed that Aurelia was helped in giving birth to her son through an obstetric section, from which the definition caesarean birth would be originated. This was certainly not the case because, had such an operation been performed, Aurelia would almost certainly have died given the total absence of antiseptic measures. This automatically rules out the possibility that complications associated with his delivery (ie obstetric traumas) might have caused him to develop any sort of childhood form of epilepsy. In addition, as J R Hughes[17] in his florid collection of facts of medical relevance (to prove that Caesar suffered from epilepsy) justly reports, 'a popular belief is that this operation can be associated with an increased incidence of seizures' – this peculiar association might explain why such a myth managed to be handed down through so many generations. Moreover, Hughes, having underlined how the story of Aurelia undergoing caesarean section might have originated in the middle ages, correctly elaborates material from the already mentioned biography of Caesar by Napoleon III of France, and recalls how the link Caesar – caesarean birth may stem from a passage found in Pliny's Natural History. '*Primusque Caesarum a caeso matris utero dictus*', 'the first of the Caesars was named after his mother's sectioned uterus' we read in the historian's work. However, it should be stressed how the name Caesar was probably of Etruscan origin, although a long list of alternative etymologies, including the Moorish word for 'elephant' (allegedly killed by one of his ancestors during the Second Punic War), has been proposed.[17]

We have now fully examined Caesar's origins: no sign of disease has been found. Moreover, Caesar was designated *Flamen Dialis* (ie the high priest of Jupiter) in 84–83 BC so, had he already been suffering from a major disease, including epilepsy, his ambitions and career might have already been endangered. This confirms the absence of any pathology at that time. Moving on to more notable clinical elements in his early life, we find in Plutarch[18] that as he was trying to escape the men of Sulla (c 138–78 BC) who wanted to kill him – he belonging to a politically opposed faction opposed to the then Roman dictator – he 'was wandering about in the country of the Sabines' and 'was changing his abode by night on account of sickness'. Caesar was finally captured by his enemies but luckily managed to persuade them to let him go. This is probably the first direct reference to a disease Caesar suffered from. The Greek text gives δι' ἀρρωστίαν [di'arrostian], literally 'on account of sickness' or 'because he was sick'. From a philological perspective this is very interesting since it can be distinguished from later references to Caesar's main disease and there does not seem to be any evidence supporting the notion that this sickness may be an early manifestation of a life-long pathological conditions. Literally ar – rostía means 'a lack of strength' thus 'a weakness', which may be looked at in the light of some rather ordinary, albeit exhausting, infectious disease, exacerbated by a status of deep stress and lack of sleep – as Suetonius specifies, he, a hunted fugitive, had to move to new a shelter 'every single night' (per singulas noctes).[19] Suetonius also gives a name to the condition that gripped the young Julius: quartana. Quartana fever is a clinical manifestation of malaria, an infectious disease caused by the pathological agent Plasmodium malariae, which cyclically presents every four days with very high body temperatures (40C or higher) and shivering. The etiology of Caesar's disease suggested by the Latin author makes great sense since malaria was very widespread in the ancient Mediterranean world, being eminently endemic in the city of Rome itself and in the surrounding Campagna until the twentieth century when scientific advances in control, prevention and pharmacological treatment made effective eradication of this historical scourge an achievable goal.[20] In his medical encyclopaedia, Aulus Cornelius Celsus (c 25 BC–c 50 AD) uses the following words to describe quartana, to which he dedicates a fascinating paragraph describing the classical alternation of cold and heat and the timing of this condition: 'Now quartan fevers have the simpler characteristics. Nearly always they begin with shivering, then heat breaks out, and the fever having ended, there are two days free; on the fourth day it recurs.'[21]

A few paragraphs later he goes on giving a complete and persuasive description of the prognosis and treatment of the condition: 'For a quartan kills no one, but when a quotidian is made out of it, the patient is in a bad way; this, however, does not happen unless through the fault either of the patient or of the practitioner.'[22]

We can well acknowledge that the Romans had a clear understanding of the clinical presentation of malaria and that, being aware of the fact that it was mostly a non–life-threatening condition, had come to develop fairly good strategies to effectively cope with it and ensure a complete recovery. In the modern world, in regions such as sub–Saharan Africa, where malaria is endemic, young patients who survive experience a greatly increased risk of cognitive and neurological impairment, behavioural deficits, agitation, psychosis, epilepsy and even coma. Epileptic seizures are known to increase with parasitemia (a quantitative increase in the number of parasites in the blood) and they are especially common after childhood cerebral malaria, rocketing to as high as eighty per cent of hospital admissions. This makes malaria the principal cause of childhood neurological infirmity in those regions.[23]

So, could this early disease have had any conspicuous part to play in the major clinical condition that would affect the Roman dictator later in life? If he really had epilepsy, could this be nothing less than a long term complication of the quartana he had when he was still a young man? Could it even be added to the long list of proposed potential etiologies of his purported epilepsy? To be fairly honest, it is impossible to answer this question with a high degree of confidence, nevertheless Caesar appears to have lived a perfectly fit and healthy life until he grew somewhat old, namely when entering the last and most politically and militarily exciting phase of his career as a statesman. There is no indication whatsoever in the available sources that he experienced any complication, either systemic or strictly neurological, in the years following the episode described by Suetonius and Plutarch, hence the idea that such long-term effects of malaria showed up roughly three decades after the time of his flight from Sulla's men seems very unlikely. In a historical reassessment of Caesar's escape from Sulla, Ronald T Ridley[24] dwells upon this quartana episode endeavouring to frame it into a broader analysis of the Roman's psychological background. Let us follow his reasoning as he recalls the alternation of symptoms malaria patients experience: 'The attacks are marked in the mild cases by four stages: cold, hot, sweating and fever-free. The cold stage is characterized by uncontrollable shivering, with perhaps nausea for as long as two hours; nothing can make the patient warm. The hot stage makes any clothing intolerable, with nausea and perhaps delirium (lasting one to eight hours). The sweating brings relief.' From this clinically accurate description he draws a captivating conclusion in an interrogative manner: 'Might we not expect anyone suffering from such a chronic but recurrent and incapacitating sickness to show certain mental signs, such as fatalism, recklessness and hyperactivity in the intervals of freedom from attack?' To support his claims Ridley mentions a case of malaria from Nigeria in a 15-year old who was extremely energetic, displaying grand delusions and constantly talking about being an important person. This case report is without doubt relevant to the discussion, but not too much should be inferred from it, and a parallel with young Caesar is not exactly accurate in that Caesar already knew himself to be, and acted as, a member of a famous, albeit decayed Roman family. His energy and mental recklessness ought not to be looked at as magnified by the effects of malaria. On the contrary, the fact that great stress and turmoil of his first years, hunted down by his Sullan political opponents and having become the head of his family prematurely because of his father's sudden demise, together with some purely psychological effects caused by the recurring symptoms of quartana, could reasonably be looked at as one of the factors that contributed to the establishment of his character and iron will.

After this episode and still running from his foes, Caesar went to Asia where he served in the army winning his first awards on account of his bravery on the battlefield, in particular receiving the civic crown decoration during the siege of Mytilene, the capital of the island of Lesbos, home to the famous poetess Sappho (c 630/612 BC–570 BC), just a few miles off the coast of modern-day Turkey. During his Asian sojourn he is said to have indulged in an amorous liaison with king Nicomedes of Bythinia (on the throne from c 94 to 74 BC): this led to enormous speculation and gossip about his sexual preferences and continence and we will analyse it thoroughly in the next chapter when assessing the possibility that he might have contracted sexually transmitted diseases that might have, in the long run, impaired his brain. Immediately afterwards, Sulla having died, Caesar moved to the Greek island of Rhodes, partially to escape revenge from political adversaries he had been battling with in court, partially intending to study rhetoric under Apollonius Molon, a famed teacher of eloquence who but a few years earlier had also taught Cicero. On his way to Rhodes, in the proximity of Pharmacusa (modern-day Farmakonisi) a very unfortunate incident troubled his plans: he was captured by the pirates who patrolled those waters and represented a huge threat to commerce and Roman authority.

Let us follow Plutarch's theatrically admirable account of the facts:

'To begin with, then, when the pirates demanded twenty talents for his ransom, he laughed at them for not knowing who their captive was, and of his own accord agreed to give them fifty. In the next place, after he had sent various followers to various cities to procure the money and was left with one friend and two attendants among Cilicians, most murderous of men, he held them in such disdain that whenever he lay down to sleep he would send and order them to stop talking. For eight and thirty days, as if the men were not his watchers, but his royal body-guard, he shared in their sports and exercises with great unconcern. He also wrote poems and sundry speeches which he read aloud to them, and those who did not admire these he would call to their faces illiterate Barbarians, and often laughingly threatened to hang them all. The pirates were delighted at this, and attributed his boldness of speech to a certain simplicity and boyish mirth. But after his ransom had come from Miletus and he had paid it and was set free, he immediately manned vessels and put to sea from the harbour of Miletus against the robbers. He caught them, too, still lying at anchor off the island, and got most of them into his power. Their money he made his booty, but the men themselves he lodged in the prison at Pergamum, and then went in person to Junius, the governor of Asia, on the ground that it belonged to him, as praetor of the province, to punish the captives. But since the praetor cast longing eyes on their money, which was no small sum, and kept saying that he would consider the case of the captives at his leisure, Caesar left him to his own devices, went to Pergamum, took the robbers out of prison, and crucified them all, just as he had often warned them on the island that he would do, when they thought he was joking.'[25]

This event gives us a superb psychological insight into Caesar's character and potently reinforces the considerations we made earlier about his upbringing and the effects – purely psychological, by no means neuropathological – of his escape from hunting when also suffering from malaria. We gather that from early adulthood Caesar proved a man of unbelievably strong mettle and that his will was already capable of enduring terrible hardships laughing in the face of danger and death, ready to cast the die committing his life to goddess Fortuna, of whom he must have patently thought to be a favourite. An equivalent to this Plutarchean passage is also encountered, albeit in epitomised form, by Suetonius. Interestingly, like when we discussed Caesar's malaria, the Roman author is once more much more precise and detailed than his Greek counterpart. Where Plutarch unspecifically writes 'was left with one friend and two attendants', Suetonius clarifies '*cum uno medico et cubiculariis duobus*', which means 'with one physician and two attendants', so we understand that one friend mentioned by Plutarch was in fact a medical person. It goes without saying that this can be of great relevance to our dissertation and it is lamentable that even the best and richest commentaries on Caesar's disease have for so long a time ignored it. Merit for justly directing scholarly attention to it should go to Montemurro and colleagues who highlighted it in their recently published study. They interestingly wonder, 'So, why did Caesar prefer to have a doctor at his side instead of a Roman soldier? We cannot know whether his decision was only secondary to fever, that Suetonius reported, or if he well knew he was subject to epileptic fits.'[26] These thoughts allow us to formulate three extra questions:

a. Was it his decision to have a doctor by his side or did the pirates command so?
b. In so complicated a situation who would be more helpful, a medical doctor or one soldier?
c. Does Caesar's behaviour on the island at the pirates' court in the following days point anyhow to a condition of physical and mental incapacity and infirmity which would justify the presence of a physician?

Let's answer them step by step. Question *a* does not have a straightforward answer and the original words do not help since the Latin is *mansitque* 'and he stayed, and he remained', while the Greek expressed this with the participle ἀπολελειμμένος [apoleleimménos] 'left'. So one is 'left' somewhere if others are sent away from him or if, he having taken that decision in the first place, finds himself in the condition of now being deprived of those who have taken leave of him. Similarly, 'he stayed', even if apparently showing Caesar himself acting so, may only be the result of the fact his friends had left. In this case philology and grammar are no great help, yet we may assume that the decision was agreed on by the two parties, the pirates being at one time advantaged by their military superiority and weakened by their prisoner's bold enticements and offer of a huge ransom, way more than they had asked for (fifty talents instead of twenty, a huge sum in those days).

Question *b* seems rather easy to answer with a question in return: would one soldier, even fully armed, perfectly trained and fearless ever be able to protect his young master from harm or torture when he was held prisoner by a vast number of bandits? Certainly not and it is unlikely they would have in any case allowed armed enemies to be on the island. A physician could be much more useful and take care of Julius Caesar during his captivity.

Finally question *c*. On the island Caesar behaved in a very bold way. As we read in Plutarch, he would give speeches, write poems and would make fun of the pirates. This means he was in perfect mental and physical conditions. While he could have penned something even if suffering from some sickness, his vigour and energy testify to his good health. The doctor's presence on the island may simply be a coincidence. He was probably allowed to choose somebody from his crew who could be of help in the event of being maltreated or getting some disease in that inhospitable place. In any case, given the pirates' expectations about the rich ransom, it would not have been wise for them to kill Caesar or harm him very much – rather, it would have made sense in terms of later saving their own lives, but that exceeds the scope of our assessment. In sum, persevering in the misconception that some neurological disease, either derived from malaria or some early manifestation of epilepsy, might have gripped Caesar already at this stage just won't do.

It is now time to analyse Caesar's first complete moral and physical descriptions as reported by his two main biographers, since they allow us to get a general idea of the ancients' perception of his health.

Suetonius reports:

'He is said to have been **tall of stature** [*excelsa statura*] with a **fair complexion** [*colore candido*], **shapely limbs** [*teretibus membris*], **a somewhat full face** [*ore paulo pleniore*], **and keen black eyes** [*nigris vegetisque oculis*], **sound of health** [*valitudine prospera*], **except that towards the end he was subject to sudden fainting fits and to nightmare as well** [*nis quod tempore extremo repente animo linqui atque etiam per somnum exterreri solebat*]. **He was twice attacked by the falling sickness during his campaigns** [*comitiali quoque morbo bis inter res agendas correptus est*]. He was somewhat over-nice in the care of his person, being not only carefully trimmed and shaved, but even having superfluous hair plucked out, as some have charged; while **his baldness was a disfigurement that would trouble him greatly**, since he found that it was **often the subject of the gibes** of his detractors. Because of it he used to comb forward his scanty locks from the crown of his head, and of all the honours voted him by the senate and people there was none which he received or made use of more gladly than the privilege of wearing a laurel wreath at all times. They say, too, that he was remarkable in his dress; that he wore a senator's tunic with fringed sleeves reaching to the wrist, and always had a girdle over it, though rather a loose one; and this, they say, was the occasion of Sulla's mot, when he often warned the nobles to keep an eye on the ill-girt boy.'[27]

From this description we can make the following observations:

a. for most of his life he was thought to enjoy good health and nobody noticed signs of decay nor disease.
b. at the end of his life he started suffering from sudden episodes of fainting (*animo linqui*) and nightmares (*per somnum exterreri*, literally ' to be struck with fear during sleep').
c. the contrast between the two phases of his life, the pathology-free one and the pathological one, is strongly underlined by the words *nisi quod*, 'except that'.

d. the *morbus comitialis*, the disease causing sudden falls in the assembly hall – thus causing the meetings to be interrupted because it was interpreted as a bad omen – was recorded twice in his life during military campaigns. This disease included epilepsy and has come to be associated primarily with it, but it is not exclusively referred to epileptic disease.

e. *quoque* (also) would seem to characterise this *morbus comitialis* as something different from the faints *(animo linqui)* described above, something to be added to the pathological list, although the symptoms of fainting would fit *morbus comitialis*, too.

Plutarch's account is a little different and adds some information:

'Such spirit and ambition Caesar himself created and cultivated in his men, in the first place, because he showed, by his unsparing bestowal of rewards and honours, that he was not amassing wealth from his wars for his own luxury or for any life of ease, but that he treasured it up carefully as a common prize for deeds of valour, and had no greater share in the wealth than he offered to the deserving among his soldiers; and in the second place, by willingly undergoing every danger and refusing no toil. Now, at his love of danger his men were not astonished, knowing his ambition; but that he should undergo toils beyond his body's apparent powers of endurance amazed them, because **he was of a spare habit, had a soft and white skin, suffered from distemper in the head** [τὴν κεφαλὴν νοσώδης], **and was subject to epileptic fits** [τοῖς ἐπὶ τοῖς ἐπιληπτικοῖς ἔνοχος, *toîs epileptikoîs énochos*], **a trouble which first attacked him, we are told, in Corduba** [ἐν Κορδύβῃ πρῶτον, *en Kordýbei proton*]. Nevertheless, he did not make **his feeble health** [τὴν ἀρρωστίαν, *tèn arrostían*] an excuse for soft living, but rather his military service a cure for his feeble health, since by **wearisome journeys, simple diet, continuously sleeping in the open air, and enduring hardships, he fought off his trouble and kept his body strong against its attacks.** Most of his sleep, at least, he got in cars or litters, making his rest conducive to action, and in the day-time he would have himself conveyed to garrisons, cities, or camps, one slave who was accustomed to write from dictation as he travelled sitting by his side, and one soldier standing behind him with a sword.'[28]

And he drove so rapidly that, on his first journey from Rome to Gaul, he reached the Rhone in seven days.

Specifically, Plutarch highlights here that:

a. Caesar suffered from epileptic fits specifying that the first episode occurred in Corduba, Spain.
b. Vaguely mentions some sort of headache.
c. Calls Caesar's health 'feeble' using the same word used to describe the sickness he had when escaping from Sulla, yet this time preceded by the article 'the', which means 'his sickness, his feeble health', not 'some occasional sickness'.
d. Says that Caesar responded to this feeble health with hard work and exercise which turned him into a more robust individual, both physically and mentally. From the way this reflection is put, it would seem that this condition accompanied Caesar throughout his life.

The two descriptions have without a doubt points of contact. Chronology being defective, specific symptoms varying (nightmares and faints/headaches), by reading the passages superficially the only element of solidity that one can get from these two passages is that Caesar had epilepsy, since Plutarch says 'epileptic fits' and Suetonius writes '*morbus comitialis*'. When discussing Caesar's alleged epilepsy the impression that one gets is really that most of the old and recent research has been deeply influenced by this equation. However, when compared, the two accounts are somewhat contradictory and that conclusion may be reached only by mingling them together into one longer epileptic tale.

Suetonius: Caesar enjoys good health but at the end of his life he starts experiencing psychomotor problems such as fainting and nightmares. On top of this, likely in the same period, or even earlier – but not too early otherwise his health would have not been called '*prospera*, very good' – he has two episodes of *morbus comitialis* (epilepsy or other fall-causing pathological occurrences).

Plutarch: Caesar's health has always been feeble probably because of headaches and epilepsy, the latter occurring to him in Corduba.

A question immediately arises: can the Corduba episode be dated? Yes, it can. At least four dates are possible: 69 BC (questorship), 61 BC (proconsulship), 49 BC (first phase of the civil war), 45 BC (last phase of the civil war). Since his health, albeit Plutarch's rather generalised reference to feeble health, was excellent in his youth and adulthood, 69 BC and 61 BC should be ruled out. We are left with 49 BC and 45 BC. Unfortunately, we have no description of the Corduba episode other than the Plutarchean allusion. Dio Cassius tells us that, as he was fighting Pompey's son, he was ill:

> 'Then at last Pompey withdrew entirely from Ulia and hastened to the other town with his entire army, accomplishing the desired result. For Caesar, learning of it in time, retired, as he happened to be ill'.[29]

This however cannot be the incident Plutarch is referring to in his portrait of Caesar's health since there he says that the Corduba one was the first such epileptic occurrence, but he also gives us the description of another episode, occurred during the battle of Thapsus (northern Africa):

> 'This is the account which some give of the battle; others, however, say that Caesar himself was not in the action, but that, as he was marshalling and arraying his army, **his usual sickness** [τὸ σύνηθες νόσημα, τὸ *sýnethes nósema*] **laid hold of him**, and he, at once **aware that it was beginning, before his already wavering senses were altogether confounded and overpowered by the malady**, was carried to a neighbouring tower, where he stayed quietly during the battle.'[30]

Of the men of consular and praetorial rank who escaped from the battle, some slew themselves at the moment of their capture, and others were put to death by Caesar after capture.

Since the battle of Thapsus took place in 46 BC, the 45 BC illness mentioned by Dio Cassius, is not the first episode mentioned by Plutarch. We are then left with 49 BC as the most likely date for the Corduba episode. At the time he was 51 years old. Plutarch says that this was his usual sickness/disease, thus we should infer that he is referring to the epilepsy he mentioned in the general description. Other sources, however, like the *Bellum Africum*, suggest that Caesar took part in the battle.[31] The symptoms described, however, have been interpreted as an example of the aura warning some patients have of the imminence of a scizure.[32]

These two episodes are the ones traditionally mentioned to support the diagnosis of epilepsy in Julius Caesar and if Suetonius' words are to be believed when he writes that Caesar was seized by the *morbus comitialis* twice, then Corduba (49 BC) and Thapsus (46 BC) should be them. More episodes suggestive of *morbus comitialis*/epilepsy (according to the received interpretation) are to be found analysing Caesar's behaviour mostly after the victory in Spain in 45 BC, as he was administering power in Rome. This episode could well fit into what Suetonius refers to as '*extremo tempore animo linqui* etc' and consist mainly of psychological/psychiatric manifestations. Historically they happen in what Luciano Canfora has described has the season of the excessive honours given to Caesar in order to make the people hate him, thus paving the way for the final assassination.[33] All these episodes have a predominant behavioural component and not all of them necessarily represent pathological manifestations and may well be exhibitions of Caesar's growing power and disregard for the Republican institutions. Nonetheless they show a certain extravagance previously unknown to Caesar as well as a change in his mood and manners – he is now much more short-tempered and angry. We list them in order for the readers to get a better picture.

a. Reaction to Cicero's oration in defence of Ligarius

In 46 BC, after Caesar's victory in Africa, Cicero skilfully defends – in front of Caesar himself – the soldier Quintus Ligarius who is accused of crimes in Africa. This is the description Plutarch makes of the event in his *Life of Cicero*:

> 'It is said also that when Quintus Ligarius was under prosecution because he had been one of the enemies of Caesar, and Cicero was his advocate, Caesar said to his friends: 'What is to prevent our hearing a speech from Cicero after all this while, since Ligarius has long been

adjudged a villain and an enemy?' But when Cicero had begun to speak and was moving his hearers beyond measure, and his speech, as it proceeded, showed varying pathos and amazing grace, **Caesar's face often changed colour** [πολλὰς μὲν ἰέναι χρόας ἐπὶ τοῦ προσώπου, *pollàs mèn hiénai chróas epì toû prosópou*] **and it was manifest that all the emotions of his soul were stirred**; and at last, when the orator touched upon the struggles at Pharsalus, **he was so greatly affected that his body shook** [τιναχθῆναι τῷ σώματι, *tinachthênai tô sómati*] **and he dropped from his hand** [τῆς χειρὸς ἐκβαλεῖν, *tês cheiròs ekbaleîn*] **some of his documents**. At any rate he acquitted Ligarius under compulsion.'[34]

Cicero was undoubtedly the greatest orator of his day, yet Caesar's behaviour was rather strange and this may well be interpreted in the light of psychomotor activity. Benediktson, for instance, thinks that 'the behaviour of Caesar perfectly describes a petit mal seizure: sick appearance, loss of muscular control and coordination, shaking.'[35]

b. Appointing Caninius Revilius consul for one day

One of the consuls, Quintus Fabius Maximus, has deceased suddenly and his post should remain vacant for a few hours, nonetheless as Plutarch reports:

> 'Therefore, when Maximus the consul died, he appointed Caninius Revilius consul for the one day still remaining of the term of office. To him, as we are told, many were going with congratulations and offers of escort, whereupon Cicero said: 'Let us make haste, or else the man's consulship will have expired.'[36]

This is likely the least pathologically relevant of these incidents, yet one fails to understand why Caesar, so brilliant a strategist, would upset the senate with so ridiculous and pointless an appointment. Indeed, by doing so he was showing everyone his growing power and the fact that such offices were no longer important now that he was the sole ruler in Rome, but does it not seem a little too extravagant a decision?

c. My name is Caesar

Somebody calls Caesar 'king'. The dictator is stunned by these words and visibly annoyed replies that they should not call him that.

Plutarch writes:

'And yet those who were advocating this honour for Caesar actually spread abroad among the people a report that from the Sibylline books it appeared that Parthia could be taken if the Romans went up against it with a king, but otherwise could not be assailed; and as Caesar was coming down from Alba into the city they ventured to hail him as king. But at this the people were confounded, and Caesar, disturbed in mind, said that his name was not King, but Caesar, and seeing that his words produced an universal silence, he passed on with no very cheerful or contented looks.'[37]

Was this an ordinary manifestation of annoyance? Did Caesar perceive that in calling him 'king', his adversaries were trying to make people hate him more? Nobody questions that, yet can the angry reaction be explained purely in terms of stress? Does it not look very short-tempered?

d. Not standing up as the senators approach him / Rostra – Temple of Venus Genitrix incident

Multiple versions of this story exist and they highlight interesting aspects of Caesar's behaviour and reactions.

Plutarch reports:

'Moreover, after sundry extravagant honours had been voted him in the senate, it chanced that he was **sitting above the rostra**, and as the praetors and consuls drew near, with the whole senate following them, **he did not rise to receive them**, but as if he were dealing with mere private persons, replied that his honours needed curtailment rather than enlargement. This vexed not only the senate, but also the people, who felt that in the persons of the senators the state was insulted, and in a terrible dejection they went away at once, all who were not obliged to remain.'[38]

This actually looks like a sign of contempt for the Republican institutions, something along the lines of his appointment of a new consul just for one day, yet Plutarch's story continues:

> 'So that Caesar too, when he was aware of his mistake, immediately turned to go home, and **drawing back his toga from his neck, cried in loud tones** to his friends that he was **ready to offer his throat to anyone who wished to kill him.**'[39]

Caesar has an angry reaction, completely losing his temper. He had remained calm in much more worrisome situations, when everything could be lost such as at Alesia or Dyrrachium, but he loses his temper now. Afterwards, Plutarch makes a direct allusion to Caesar's disease, actually having the dictator justify his behaviour in front of the senate with it. He admits to being sick:

> 'But afterwards he made his disease an excuse for his behaviour, saying that **the senses** of those who are thus afflicted **do not usually remain steady when they address a multitude standing**, but are **speedily shaken and whirled about**, bringing on **giddiness** and **insensibility.**'[40]

Plutarch eventually concludes that:

> '[…]what he said was not true; on the contrary, he was very desirous of rising to receive the senate; but one of his friends, as they say, or rather one of his flatterers, Cornelius Balbus, restrained him, saying: 'Remember that thou art Caesar, and permit thyself to be courted as a superior.'[41]

In any case, even if the disease had not played its part in his failure to stand up, this story still highlights that:

a. Caesar had an abnormal reaction after the episode, showing an outburst of anger and despair and losing his temper;

b. He admits to having a disease, of which he gives a description, but does not refer to it with a specific name.

Suetonius' and Appian's versions differ a little from Plutarch's, since the Roman author places the episode in the Temple of Venus Genitrix, rather than in the Rostra. They do not specifically mention any disease.
Suetonius:

'When the Senate approached him in a body with many highly honorary decrees, he received them before the temple of Venus Genetrix **without rising**. Some think that when he attempted to get up, he was held back by Cornelius Balbus; others, that he made no such move at all, but on the contrary frowned angrily on Gaius Trebatius when he suggested that he should rise.'[42]

Appian:

'While he was thus transacting business in front of the rostra, the Senate, preceded by the consuls, each one in his robes of office, brought the decree awarding him the honours aforesaid. He extended his hand to them, but did not rise when they approached nor while they remained there, and this, too, afforded his slanderers a pretext for accusing him of wishing to be greeted as a king. He accepted all the honours conferred upon him except the ten-year consulship.'[43]

Dio Cassius, specifying that the episode took place in the Rostra, adds some pathological information, saying that some justified his decision not to rise as being the result of an attack of diarrhoea. He also adds, however, that he went home alone without major problems:

'Indeed, when once they had voted to him on a single day an unusually large number of these honours of especial importance – which had been granted unanimously by all except Cassius and a few others, who became famous for this action, yet suffered no harm, whereby Caesar's clemency was conspicuously revealed – they then approached him as he was sitting in the vestibule of the temple of Venus in order to announce to him in a body their decisions; for they transacted such business in his absence, in order to have the appearance of doing it, not under compulsion, but voluntarily. And either by some heaven-sent fatuity or even through excess of joy he received them sitting, which aroused so great indignation among them all, not only the senators but all the rest, that it afforded his slayers one of their chief excuses for their plot against him. Some who subsequently tried to defend him claimed, it is true, that owing to **an attack of diarrhoea he could not control the movement of his bowels and so had remained where he was in order to avoid a flux**. They were not able, however, to convince the majority, since **not long afterwards he rose up and went home on foot**; hence most men suspected him of being inflated with pride and hated him for his haughtiness, when it was they themselves who had made him disdainful by the exaggerated character of their honours'.[44]

Nicolaus of Damascus also gives his version of the facts, but his account is too apologetic in saying that Caesar was busy not to realise the senators were approaching him:

'Caesar was seated while they advanced and because he was conversing with men standing to one side, he did not turn his head toward the approaching procession or pay any attention to it, but continued to prosecute the business which he had on hand, until one of his friends, nearby, said: 'Look at these people coming up in front of you.' Then Caesar laid down his papers and turned around and listened to what they had to say.'[45]

Did Caesar not stand up because he was really having an episode of his disease? Or was he just offending the senate? If the second eventuality is what happened how to consider his angry reaction once at home and his own description of his disease?

e. Friction with the Tribune Pontius Aquila

Caesar did not stand up when the senators approached him, yet he is said not to have forgiven Pontius Aquila, a tribune, for not rising in his presence. His reaction on the spot and during the following days was quite extreme and angry. Was this purely an example of struggle for power? Why was Caesar so short-tempered?

Suetonius writes:

'[…] when he himself in one of his triumphal processions rode past the benches of the tribunes, he was so incensed because a member of the college, Pontius Aquila, did not rise, that **he cried**: 'Come then, Aquila, take back the republic from me, you tribune'; and for several days he would not make a promise to anyone without adding, 'That is, if Pontius Aquila will allow me.'[46]

f. Fury at the tribunes Flavius and Marullus

Laurel crowns are put on his statues. Two tribunes have them removed but Caesar's reaction is furious.

Suetonius:

'To an insult which so plainly showed his contempt for the Senate he added an act of even greater insolence; for at the Latin Festival, as he was returning to the city, amid the extravagant and unprecedented demonstrations of the populace, someone in the press placed on his statue a laurel wreath with a white fillet tied to it; and when Epidius Marullus and Caesetius Flavius, tribunes of the commons, gave orders that the ribbon be removed from the wreath and the man taken off to prison, Caesar sharply rebuked and deposed them, either offended that the hint at regal power had been received with so little favour, or, as he asserted, that he had been robbed of the glory of refusing it.'[47]

Plutarch and Dio Cassius better describe Caesar's anger and subsequent reaction, when he insults the people:

'So two of the tribunes, Flavius and Maryllus, went up to them and pulled off the diadems, and after discovering those who had first hailed Caesar as king, led them off to prison. Moreover, the people followed the tribunes with applause and called them Brutuses, because Brutus was the man who put an end to the royal succession and brought the power into the hands of the senate and people instead of a sole ruler. At this, Caesar was greatly vexed, and deprived Maryllus and Flavius of their office, while in his denunciation of them, although **he at the same time insulted the people, he called them repeatedly Brutes and Cymaeans**.'[48]

Dio Cassius:

'And when the tribunes, Gaius Epidius Marullus and Lucius Caesetius Flavius, took it down, he became violently angry, although they uttered no word of abuse and moreover actually praised him before the populace as not wanting anything of the sort. For the time being, though vexed, he held his peace.'[49]

g. The Lupercalia Incident

On 15 February 44 BC Rome is celebrating its festivity called the Lupercalia.[50] Mark Antony offers Caesar a crown, which he refuses several times. Reaction in the crowd is varied, some applaud, and others ask him to accept the title of king. Some schools of thought posit that it was his idea to try this in public in order to test people's reaction, others believe that it was Antony's idea or even an attempt to destabilise Caesar's power.

In his *Life of Antony* Plutarch reports Caesar's angry reaction, which is very similar to the one described in the *Life of Caesar*, as he goes back home after not standing up to honour the senators:

'At last Caesar **rose** from the rostra **in displeasure, and pulling back the toga from his throat cried out that anyone who pleased might smite him there**. The wreath, which had been hung upon one of his statues, certain tribunes of the people tore down. These men the people greeted with favouring cries and clapping of hands; but Caesar deprived them of their office.'[51]

Caesar is evidently described again as short-tempered and quick to anger. No further information is given about potential changes to his complexion, nor about trembling, yet given the rage of the moment, that's a possibility. Again, was this a normal reaction, or something suggesting a pathological background?

h. Epilepsy caused by inactivity?

In the second book of his work on the Civil War, Appian, approaching the end of his account of Caesar's life, makes a rather general statement on his health and suggests that he was epileptic, adding that he planned on the huge campaign against the Parthians and Getae to cure his disease. However, given the context in which it is said, it would appear that the disease also refers to the last phase of his life:

> 'And now Caesar, either renouncing his hope, or being tired out, and wishing by this time to avoid this plot and odium, or deliberately giving up the city to certain of his enemies, or hoping to cure his bodily ailment of epilepsy and convulsions [εἴτε νόσημα τοῦ σώματος θεραπεύων, ἐπιληψίαν καὶ σπασμὸν αἰφνίδιον ἐμπίπτοντα αὐτῷ μάλιστα παρὰ τὰς ἀργίας, eíte nósema toû sómatos therapeúon, epilepsían kaì spasmòn aiphnídion empíptonta autô málista para tàs argías], which came upon him suddenly and especially when he was inactive, conceived the idea of a long campaign against the Getae and the Parthians.'[52]

The idea that he wanted to cure his epilepsy by means of a military campaign does not make sense medically. It may well be that he thought that moving away from Rome where the pressure was too great on him and where the attacks of this condition intensified – at the same time recalling his old years in Gaul when his health was fine, he dreamed of going back to such a situation, hard in terms of fighting but far from conspiracies and his late onset health issues. Nonetheless, the next passages we will examine shed more light on his final mood, characterised by a certain degree of depression.

h. Dinner in the house of Lepidus, Night before the Ides of March and morning of the assassination.

Suetonius, who had already described a major shift in Caesar's health towards the end of this life, confirms it at the end of his biography by saying that Caesar, because of his condition, appeared uninterested in living any longer:

> 'Caesar left in the minds of some of his friends the suspicion that he did not wish to live longer and had taken no precautions, because of his failing health [*Suspicionem Caesar quibusdam suorum reliquit neque voluisse se diutius vivere neque curasse quod valitudine minus prospera uteretur*]; and that therefore he neglected the warnings which came to him from portents and from the reports of his friends.'[53]

He then describes a famous episode that occurred the night before Caesar's assassination, in which he describes the kind of death he would like to have:

> 'About one thing almost all are fully agreed, that he all but desired such a death as he met; for once when he read in Xenophon how Cyrus in his last illness gave directions for his funeral, he expressed his horror of such a lingering kind of end and his wish for one which was swift and sudden. And the day before his murder, in a conversation which arose at a dinner at the house of Marcus Lepidus, as to **what manner of death was most to be desired,** he had given his preference **to one which was sudden and unexpected.**'[54]

These two passages appear to portray Caesar as being eventually disillusioned, or more frankly speaking, somewhat depressed and not necessarily willing to live any longer.

Plutarch confirms the episode:

> '[...] on the day before, when Marcus Lepidus was entertaining him at supper, Caesar chanced to be **signing letters,** as his custom was, while reclining at table, and the discourse turned suddenly upon the

question what sort of death was the best; before anyone could answer Caesar cried out: 'That which is unexpected.'[55]

Neurologically speaking, this passage is very important since there is the proof that Caesar is having a normal conversation, somehow enjoying (or pretending to) the party and he is signing letters, testifying that of all possible diseases he might have had, he had no such thing as cognitive impairment or dementia until the very end. Most historical accounts then focus on the next day, the Ides of March, yet Appian adds something more about what happens after the dinner and tells us about the bad omens that ensued:

> 'In this way he foretold his own end, and conversed about what was to happen on the morrow. After the banquet **a certain bodily faintness** [αὐτῷ τὸ σῶμα νωθρὸν ἐγίγνετο, *autô tò sôma nothròn egígneto*] came over him **in the night**, and his wife, Calpurnia, had a dream, in which she saw him streaming with blood, for which reason she tried to prevent him from going out in the morning. When he offered sacrifice there were many unfavourable signs.'[56]

This note is extremely interesting since it says that, following the dinner, Caesar does not feel well. Now, we know that they had wine the night before – the 'banquet', being called '*pothos*', thus a drinking banquet – but we also know that Caesar was very moderate in drinking, so there is no reason to believe he got drunk that night.

During the night a strange dream occurs to him, which Dio Cassius reports:

> 'For the night before he was slain his wife dreamed that their house had fallen in ruins and that her husband had been wounded by some men and had taken refuge in her bosom; **and Caesar dreamed he was raised aloft upon the clouds and grasped the hand of Jupiter.**'[57]

In the morning, then, after several bad omens, and his health not being excellent he is not sure about going to the Senate and does not feel well.

Professor Barry Strauss (combining historical and medical perspectives with the neurologist Professor Carl Bazil), in his recent book *The Death of Caesar*, examines these late events underling how they may show the possibility of an unrecognised pathological occurrence: Strauss highlights that Caesar felt sluggish after he went back home from dinner in the house of Lepidus on the night of 14 March and that he continued to feel badly the next morning – he reportedly complained about vertigo. Strauss then raises the interesting possibility that these symptoms might have been of 'an undetected epileptic seizure' and acknowledges the fact that the dizziness he experienced on that day, as well as the fainting and night terrors he is said to have experienced towards the end of his life, could be attributed in hindsight to the manifestations of an epileptic seizure.

These observations lead the scholar to the conclusion that, if that really be the case, Caesar's judgement might have been impaired on 15 March, in spite of how normal he might have appeared to be. Strauss, however, suggests prudence when analysing this episode, since, he notes, difficulties are met with when the only available evidence consists of fragmentary details from over 2,000 years ago. Strauss even considers the possibility that Caesar never really had a disease and that the symptoms attributed to him might have been invented by his own party and supporters after his death as a manner of accounting for his blindness to peril on the Ides of March.[58]

All those possibilities should be taken into account. More hints at the fact that Caesar's health might have been poor that morning can be found in the description of the moment immediately preceding his assassination in the Senate House.

Suetonius specifically stressed Caesar's poor health and reports that both this and the omens (including his wife Calpurnia's supplication to stay at home) were responsible for his failure to resolve whether he should go to the senate: 'Both for these reasons and because of poor health [*ob haec simul et ob infirmam valitudinem*] he hesitated for a long time [*diu cunctatus*] whether to stay at home and put off what he had planned to do in the senate.'[59]

However, Decimus Brutus Albinus, one of the conspirators, whom Caesar trusted, seeing that Caesar's arrival in the senate was being delayed, went to Caesar's house and persuaded him to come along with him. Caesar is patently confused and uncertain, Decimus dominates the conversation by mocking the omens and, according to Plutarch, making him believe that they are going to proclaim him king of all provinces, thus enabling him to wear a diadem everywhere outside Italy.

As he speaks thus, 'Brutus' takes 'Caesar by the hand [τῆς χειρὸς λαβόμενος τὸν Καίσαρα, *tês cheiròs labómenos tòn Kaísara*] and' begins 'to lead him along.'[60] Psychologically Caesar is patently weak and can be easily ordered about by Decimus Brutus. His willpower has gone. This strongly points to the fact that his health was very poor that morning. This, in addition, is also confirmed by the fact that he is brought to the senate, as Appian writes [φερομένουδὲ ἤδη τοῦ Καίσαρος, *pheroménou dè éde toû Kaísaros*], so it could be interpreted he needs some transportation (such as a litter) not only because he needs to hurry up since he is late but also because of his feeble condition.[61]

All these stories preceding the assassination seem to confirm that something was wrong with Caesar. Excluding Thapsus and Corduba, the major episodes, he suffered from symptoms such as dizziness, numbness, outbursts of anger, depression, etc. Some of the listed episodes may well be explained in purely political terms (specially the one involving the consulate and his reaffirming that his name was Caesar), nonetheless it would be equally wrong to look at this long and detailed sequence of events as totally free of pathological connotations, thus we are of the opinion that they should be included in the reassessment of his health.

The facts have been listed and the original sources have been consulted. Most people re-examining his life have been faced with the following data:

a. Two Greek authors (Plutarch and Appian) write that he suffered from epilepsy;
b. Suetonius mentions the *morbus comitialis*, which has been traditionally associated with epilepsy;
c. Two major episodes are mentioned (Corduba and Thapsus), one (Thapsus) even described in detail;
d. Several incidents suggestive of psychomotor changes are reported during his last years of life and these symptoms are common findings in epileptic patients;
e. He admits to having a disease which, according to his description resembles epilepsy or its psychomotor symptoms (although he does not call it 'epilepsy').

On the basis of these facts the epileptic theory became dominant and lasted for centuries, with scant attempts to question it. The theory is, however, mainly based on the assumption that Plutarch's (and Appian's) reference to 'epilepsy' matched Suetonius' '*morbus comitialis*'. With such a foundation, then, all the described episodes may as a consequence have been retrospectively tailored to rationalize an epileptic disease. We have already been analyzing the matter in detail, discarding the idea that Caesar suffered from epilepsy or other incapacitating medical conditions in his youth; we therefore started our analysis with a clean slate – attempting to clear our approach from known biases as much as possible. As the book unfolds, we will question all aspects of this epileptic assumption. As a first step, chapter two will take a close and critical look at the theories which, starting from that very assumption, speculated on the cause of this epilepsy.

Chapter Two

Looking for the Cause of Caesar's Epilepsy: A Two Thousand Year Legacy

In the previous chapter we endeavoured to collect all the existing evidence about the diseases Julius Caesar suffered throughout his life, listing them in chronological order so that the readers could get a crystal-clear picture of the ailments that gripped him, primarily, as Suetonius puts it, towards the end of his life. We have also seen how the words 'epileptic fits' used by Plutarch and '*morbus comitialis*' used by Suetonius have always been regarded as one and the same, thus providing theoretical philological background for the powerful establishment of what we refer to as 'the epileptic theory', although, given its entrenchment in the minds of historians, it justly ought to be named 'the epileptic dogma'.

Having largely accepted the premise that the disease really was epilepsy without questioning its philologico-clinical foundations, most scholars and medical researchers have moved to the next step: the identification of the real cause of his epilepsy. In strictly medical terms, they have moved their focus from semiotics onto etiology. When sources, be it literary, artistic or osteological, are scant, venturing into this specific field may prove difficult and, when shown to lack any consistency, may put the credibility of the whole pathographic reconstruction of a historical character's sufferings in doubt. Such methodological mistakes characterized old-style pathography and major criticism of it has been that it was but an idle exhibition of clinical acumen and bravura meant to paste hyper-sophisticated diagnoses – based on modern evidence-based criteria – to historical characters, irrespective of the nature, evolution and presentation and, most importantly, description of diseases in the past, thus running up against anachronistic intepretations.[1]

Nonetheless, the new pathographic approach which has been growing over the past few years and which we ourselves have tried to implement effectively for this study can be a valiant ally to both clinical and paleopathological medicine, as well as to the realm of classical research. By using primary sources alone in their original languages, putting the meaning of the analysed passages in historical context, availing oneself of both clinical and historical perspectives, it is possible to elevate the platform from which ancient diseases are contemplated and to produce interesting theoretical insights into their social and historical role.

Specifically focusing on Caesar's case, the fact that multiple sources are at hand (biographies and historical accounts written by more than one author and in different languages, as well as data from paleopathogical research covering roughly the same historical period considered) allows us to develop that basis consisting of symptoms and signs into an etiological framing. This means that formulating hypotheses on the exact cause of Caesar's disease goes far beyond what to some may appear simply an exhibition of erudite guessing or showy speculation.

This being the case, let us take a closer look at what scholars have thought might have caused Caesar's epileptic attacks, adding our personal comments and highlighting their strengths and weaknesses. To do so, a very sound and clinically rigorous approach is, rather than proceeding in chronological order and listing when and by whom certain etiological hypotheses have been put forward, to distinguish between early onset and late onset epilepsy. The former simply means that the first manifestations occur during childhood, while the latter term describes a type of epilepsy in which symptoms present much later in life.

Early onset epilepsy and epilepsy in Caesar's adolescence or very early adulthood

There is negligible evidence that Julius Caesar suffered from epilepsy in his early years. If by early onset epilepsy we mean a condition showing up during the first months of life and accompanying the patient throughout childhood, then no evidence whatsoever is to be found in the sources. Should we perhaps be of the opinion that the ancient sources have omitted reports of fits during his childhood and early years simply because at the time he was not famous? This seems a very unlikely eventuality, given the relevance of Caesar's character, especially to Plutarch, who draws a parallel with Alexander the Great. It seems likely that all biographical minutiae and early anecdotes must have been reported in order to enrich the scope of the biography.

Considering instead epilepsy manifesting in adolescence or very early adulthood, even if the Plutarchean reference to his first attack in Corduba were to be posited to have happened in 69 BC, at the time of his Spanish quaestorship, or in 61-60 BC when he was there as pro consul (therefore much earlier than dates like 49 BC when the Civil War broke out), he would have been either 31 or 38 (sticking to the accepted chronology), so already too much into adult life for him to be classified as suffering from early-onset epilepsy. To maintain such a stance, one must operate a fusion between three concepts, two specific ones, the other a little vaguer: the fact that malaria caused long-term problems in his brain, that the presence of a physician with him as he was being held captive by the pirates and that sentence found in Plutarch we looked at earlier, namely where he says that he never took his physical weakness caused by his disease as an excuse for a placid life, on the contrary judging military life the cure to such a weakness. Theoretically speaking one could do that, but, as we have seen, how would one be able then to justify the fact that no reference whatsoever is ever made to any potential cognitive impairment and that Suetonius explicitly states that Caesar's health issue started to manifest when he was approaching old age? Furthermore, does the Plutarchean passage not seem to be much too general and all-encompassing a sentence and greatly imbued with moral and ethical reflections, to be taken as a statement that over the entire course of his life Caesar suffered from a major incapacitating medical condition such as epilepsy?

The answer is evident and the sources are too scant and self-explanatory to allow anyone to uphold so ungrounded a hypotheses. Despite all of this, the neurologist J R Hughes,[2] as will be explained later (see 'Late Onset Epilepsy') chooses to incorporate the disease Caesar had while fleeing from Sulla's hired assassins into a complex hypothesis addressing a potential genetic cause.

Late Onset Epilepsy

If the epileptic theory is to be believed, this variant of epileptic disease seems to be the most likely in Julius Caesar's case. In his monumental work on 'The Falling Sickness', O Temkin wrote that it was the great Italian poet Francesco Petrarca (Petrarch, 1304–1374) who stressed this idea for the first time in his work *De remediis utriusque fortunae*. In particular Temkin quotes from an archaic English version by the Elizabethan translator and physician Thomas Twyne (1543-1613) of the following passage, which we reproduce also providing key Latin bits from the original for comparison:

> 'Here "Reason" says: Thou canst not fall into that [ie a trance] twice. For none dyeth more than once: and whiche shoulde be the best kynde of death, there was sometyme disputation among certayne learned and notable men, at whiche was Iulius Caesar in presence, for empire and learnyng a most excellent personage: who also in his latter tyme, as some wryte of hym, used many tymes to faynt suddeynly [*qui et ipse tempore extremo, ut de illo scriptum est, repente linqui animo solebat*], which question he in this manner determined, concludyng, that a suddeine and unlookedfor death, as of al the most commodious.'[3]

In order to present the different etiologies clearly, the International League Against Epilepsy (ILAE) classification, put in a schematic form, is very helpful. It lists two major groups: generalized and focal epilepsy. The former alludes to what is also known as 'primary generalized' or 'idiopathic' epilepsy. This means that the epilepsy is the primary disease and not a symptomatic consequence of some other medical condition. The latter, also known as partial epilepsy/seizure, on the other hand, refers to a kind of impaired electrical activity which starts and remains limited in a specific area of the brain – although such alteration in the transmission of the electrical signal in the brain has the potential to become generalized in a successive phase, in which eventuality the correct definition becomes 'secondary generalized'. It is the consequence of other forms of insult (ie damage) to the brain, thus it is secondary in essence.

Thus:

- **Primary** or **Generalized** = epilepsy is the primary disease.[4]
- **Secondary** or **Partial** or **Focal** = epilepsy is only the consequence of another brain disease.

With this clearer picture in mind, it becomes much easier to classify the potential etiologies by means of stuffing, so to speak, those two very broad categories. For the sake of clarity and avoiding confusion caused by too specialised medical terminology, we shall only use primary and secondary epilepsy to refer to the groups above.

Late onset epilepsy
As briefly touched upon above, this theory is strongly supported by the neurologist Professor J R Hughes in his 2004 publication in the respected medical journal *Epilepsy and Behaviour*. Its roots may well be identified in the old tradition which looks at the Julio-Claudian dynasty as a whole stemming from the great Julius, the Pater Patriae and Divus, whose virtues, vices, predispositions and diseases must have been passed on to his descendants, including the infamous Caligula and Nero, whose alleged follies still stand out as examples of a wicked exploitation of power and have become synonymous with evil and tyrannical rule. Unlike historians of old (and, why not, contemporary ones), who might well have written about their rulers *cum ira et studio* (ie with anger and partisanship – so much for Tacitus' prefatory statement of being *sine*, 'without'!), as scientists know, genes generally do not lie. This is certainly more of an established notion for organic diseases (including neurological conditions), rather than for psychiatric ones and even more so for normal or border-line psychological traits, on which an exuberant number of studies is still working to provide medicine with a clearer understanding of the facts.

Corroborated by this background, following in the footsteps of D T Benediktson and stressing the word '*spasmos*' used by Appian to describe Caesar's fits,[5] Hughes suggests that what the dictator experienced were 'absence attacks'. These attacks, also known by the archaic French definition of '*petit mal seizures*' (little illness), represent brief losses of consciousness, from which the patient generally recovers quickly. As specified above, such epileptic seizures are generalized, that is, not limited to one single area, they involve both cerebral hemispheres from the onset. Elaborating on this observation, Hughes correctly reports that such crises are 'clearly the most frequently inherited type' and also underlines that the fashion of inheritance has been hypothetised to be either autosomal dominant (ie caused by a single dominant allele, or gene variety) or more complex. He then focuses his attention on the episode of Sulla's attempt to assassinate him narrated by Plutarch and interprets that 'on account of sickness' as 'possible seizures [...] because we know of no other health problems except the 'falling sickness' (or possibly, but unlikely, malaria)'.

The fact that malaria may be unlikely seems a little peculiar, to say the least. As we have seen in the first chapter, it suffices to peruse Suetonius' account of the same episode to see that he clearly names it '*quartana*', the quartan ague. We have also stressed the fact that the area around Rome, large portions of Southern Italy and Rome itself were endemic regions for malaria. One may well speculate that Caesar might have developed some form of immunity as is the case with individuals being born in regions where malaria is endemic and that, unlike a foreigner coming from a totally malaria-free part of the world, he might have experienced a less potent and debilitating form of that disease and might well have survived, but to call the possibility of malaria 'unlikely' does not seems to respect the historical epidemiological data from those lands.

Caesar's father and great-grandfather. Medically analysing Caesar's relatives further, Hughes correctly focuses his attention on his father and great-grandfather and to their purported sudden deaths, as reported by Plinius in his *Natural History*. 'To make a stronger case for inheritance' – Hughes writes – 'there is a need to show that the ancestors of Julius Caesar also had epilepsy.' He later affirms that the evidence 'is not clear that either of them had epilepsy', having a moment before given his opinion on such a lamentable lack of information: 'none of them was sufficiently famous to have inspired detailed biographies'. He then concludes that 'there is no justification to state that those deaths were sudden unexpected death in epilepsy (SUDEP)'– yet 'this diagnosis cannot be excluded and remains a possibility'.

Let's look closer at what SUDEP, a tragic complication of epileptic disease, is. It is defined as 'sudden, unexpected, witnessed or unwitnessed, non-traumatic, and non-drowning death in a patient with epilepsy.' Its cause is still uncertain and several etiologies, including pulmonary, strictly neurological or cardiological have been suggested. Its frequency is higher in the range 20-40 years, men being more likely than women to be affected and the risk of developing it has been found to be higher in individuals having frequent seizures and taking large doses of many anti-epileptic drugs.[6]

Speaking of frequencies and likelihood, there is no shared consensus on the incidence of SUDEP and it should be stressed that its social burden may have been underestimated and only recently reconsidered properly. Nonetheless statistics report an 'overall crude annual incidence rate of 0.81 cases per 100,000 population, or 1.16 cases per 1,000 patients with epilepsy'.[7] As far as the ancient world is concerned, sadly we have no information whatsoever on the epidemiology of SUDEP. In the case of Caesar's ancestors only the fact that they were males complies with the above given risk factors for SUDEP. In fact they did not necessarily fit the age range for the highest incidence likelihood with Caesar's father being 55 years old when he passed away in 85 BC. Lucius Julius Caesar, being praetor in 166 BC when he died while on duty, must have been at least 39 years old since that was the age required to access the praetorship. Even if he managed to access this position one or two years earlier, sticking to a discourse on age, we would still have two purported cases of SUDEP of which one is by 15 years out of the highest incidence range, the other one is borderline. In addition, if they had suffered from severe forms of seizures of epileptic nature as is a common background for patients dying of SUDEP – maybe not to enrich their rather obscure biographies – but at least one mention of this should be present in the ancient sources since it would have been so easy to link evident manifestations of epilepsy in his ancestors, to Caesar's disease. On the contrary, even when *morbus comitialis* or those Plutarchean epileptic fits/attacks are mentioned, no reference at all is made to anything of neurological relevance in his ancestors other than their sudden deaths. Finally, epilepsy having only been really understood and effectively treated in recent times, the use of large doses of several epileptic medications should be considered, thus one of the risk factors for SUDEP can be automatically ruled out.

Hughes has the incontestable and commendable merit of having introduced the concept of inheritance to the debate by focusing on Julius's ancestors and we will fully cover this aspect when expounding our own theory. The conclusions he draws in this case are, however, open to debate. Firstly, if there is no indication that Caesar's forebears suffered from epilepsy, how can one suggest that they died of a highly specific and quite rare complication of it, merely on the basis that one of their descendants allegedly suffered from epilepsy? In addition, how, if both of them were killed by SUDEP did no other member of the family, including Julius Caesar himself, have it? Of course, clinical presentations are not an exact science and great variability exists, nevertheless the SUDEP hypothesis appears something of an over-complication, meant or interpreted to sustain the 'genetic stance'. Moreover, while we agree on the possibility that those two ancestors were not the object of detailed biographies, because of their marginal role in Roman politics and history, and we can certainly concede that the information we have on them may be due to their being related to a much more famous descendant, why then do we have such a precise description of their deaths? Indeed, details may not lie in the abundance of words used to describe those incidents, but the very fact that – given their historical irrelevance – they are mentioned and that the already discussed word *exanimatus* is adopted bears great relevance to the discussion and defines the account as detailed enough to draw some sensible conclusions.

Caesar's daughter Julia. Afterwards Hughes pays attention to the rest of the family, starting with his daughter Julia and son Caesarion. Very limited information is known about Julia (76–54 BC): Caesar had her during his first marriage with Cornelia Cinna Minor (c. 97–69 BC); she was educated by Caesar's mother Aurelia since Cornelia had died prematurely during delivery (69 or 68 BC); as her father wished it, she had to marry Pompey the Great (106 – 48 BC) in 59 BC, when he was still a political ally. She passed away in 54 BC after giving birth to an heir who did not survive her mother.

Let us follow literally what the sources report, starting from Plutarch's *Life of Pompey*:

> 'It once happened that at an election of aediles people came to blows,
> and many were killed in the vicinity of Pompey and he was covered
> with their blood, so that he changed his garments. His servants carried
> these garments to his house with much confusion and haste, and his
> young wife, who chanced to be with child, at sight of the blood-stained
> toga, fainted away and with difficulty regained her senses, and in

consequence of the shock and her sufferings, miscarried. Thus it came to pass that even those who found most fault with Pompey's friendship for Caesar could not blame him for the love he bore his wife. However, she conceived again and gave birth to a female child, but died from the pains of travail, and the child survived her only a few days.'[8]

From this story we gather that before fatally giving birth to her child, Julia had already miscarried and that upon that occasion the sight of blood had caused her a shock capable of making her faint and lose consciousness. This means that powerful stimulations such as emotionally charged events like the sight of blood or the fear of violence were an ordinary and common cause of fainting for Julia.

Valerius Maximus (a first century AD Roman author) also reports on Julia's death:

'A similar turmoil has been noted for Julia, the daughter of C. Caesar, who, having seen her husband Pompey the Great's garment soaked in blood being brought home from the Campus Martius from the election of the aediles, stunned by fear that any violence may have been done onto him, unconscious she fell to the ground and because of the sudden psychological shock and great physical pain was forced to expel the birth, which she had conceived in her womb, certainly to the great detriment of the whole world, whose peace would have not been disturbed by the rage of so many bloody civil wars, if Caesar and Pompey's common harmony had remained tied together by a bond of blood.'[9]

This account is similar to Plutarch's, yet there is one substantial point of divergence. While Plutarch says that the sight of blood caused Julia to faint and give birth prematurely, he does not link this episode with her death. On the contrary, he states that this happened later. He also adds some information on the sex of the new-born, clearly affirming that it was a female. Valerius Maximus on the contrary, avoids giving any information on whether the child was male or female and melds the two stories into one account, which does not support the observation (derived from Plutarch) that such strong emotional shocks were a very common cause of potent distress in Julia.

The Roman author Velleius Paterculus also mentions Julia's death:

'About the fourth year of Caesar's stay in Gaul occurred the death of Julia, the wife of Pompey, the one tie which bound together Pompey and Caesar in a coalition which, because of each one's jealousy of the other's power, held together with difficulty even during her lifetime; and, as though fortune were bent upon breaking all the bonds between the two men destined for so great a conflict, Pompey's little son by Julia also died a short time afterwards.'[10]

This description does not offer many more details than the previous ones. Like Valerius Maximus, Velleius Paterculus agrees on the fact that Julia's sudden demise ruined a fragile political pact between Caesar and Pompey, thus paving the way for civil war. Apart from such historical reflections, we understand that the child she gave birth to was a son, not a daughter as in Plutarch's passage.

Looking for epilepsy, no certain information can be inferred from these accounts and Hughes correctly admits that 'we can only speculate that the miscarriage and her death in childbirth, in addition to the child's death, had any relevance to seizures. Nothing else is known about her.' In a 1912 article in the *Glasgow Medical Journal* Dr Kanngiesser, re-examining the accounts seen above, in particular Valerius Maximus and Velleius, made the following interrogative reflections: '*Partus immaturus*, etiology: shock? Eclampsia? Epilepsy? A case of recurring *vertigo epileptica ex aspectu sanguinis* is personally known to me.'[11]

Let's look at those words – apart from epilepsy, which we should have at this point understood enough about. *Shock* is a potentially life-threatening clinical condition in which low blood perfusion to tissues results in damage to cells and subsequent ineffective tissue function. It can be caused by several factors including cardiac and endocrine problems, but also by very strong emotional distress. *Eclampsia* is the onset of convulsions in a woman who already has *pre-eclampsia*, a condition characteristic of pregnancy in which there is hypertension, edema and a large amount of protein is found in the urine (proteinuria). A severe complication of *pre-eclampsia* is the so-called HELLP syndrome, consisting of haemolysis (destructions of red blood cells), elevated liver enzymes and low platelet count: in a certain number of patients disseminated intravascular coagulation can cause death and if epileptic seizures arise this can mean a progression to full-blown *eclampsia*.

Eclampsia can cause severe problems or even death through kidney or liver failure. Moreover, since coagulation may be impaired, a haemolytic-uremic syndrome (IIUS), consisting of haemolytic anaemia, thrombocytopenia (decreased blood platelets) and acute kidney failure. All these relevant medical issues still represent a problem even in societies where medicine is advanced and effective treatments are available and are a key cause of death in women in developing countries. *Recurring vertigo epileptica ex aspectu sanguinis* means 'recurring epileptic vertigo caused by the sight of blood': the expression is very confusing since vertigo was used as a synonym of *petit mal* epilepsy in the past and very much differs from our modern use of the word. In any case, Kanngiesser is speculating that two etiologies may be responsible for Julia's premature delivery and death: *eclampsia* and some manifestation of epilepsy associated with a powerful stimulus such as the sight of her husband's blood. Did Julia have some form of epilepsy inherited from her father Julius? The evidence appears to be somewhat scant and circumstantial. Did she have *eclampsia*? Given her agitation we may speculate that, since she was pregnant, she had hypertension caused either by *pre-eclampsia* or *eclampsia* and that episodes like the sight of blood or violence simply exacerbated her distress by means a potent neurocardiogenic syncope (a sudden and transient loss of consciousness with spontaneous recovery) which has been reported in association with *pre-eclampsia*. In chapter one we commented on the fact that Julia's mother, too, died while delivering a child. Given her father's historical prominence scholars tend to look at him as the genetic 'vector' and 'transmitter' of the disease from which she might have suffered and died, but attention should equally be paid to her mother. This allows us to consider the inheritability of *pre-eclampsia* and *eclampsia* which has been suggested in some clinical studies and evidence has been put forward, although a crystal-clear mode of inheritance has not been designed so far, since the condition is a complex disorder and several genes are involved in its genesis. This could more logically explain Julia's fainting and premature delivery, without necessarily looking for a complicated and rather rare recurring epileptic vertigo that she might have inherited from her father Julius.

Caesarion. (Accepted dates: 47 BC–30 BC). Julius Caesar's invasion of Egypt chasing Pompey after he had crushed him at Pharsalus and his love affair with Cleopatra (69–30 BC) is a very well-known chapter of Roman and Mediterranean, if not world, history. This union would provoke great indignation in Rome since the old senatorial class saw in it more hard evidence for Caesar's dream going far beyond the idea of dictatorship and military command over the Republic. They thought he was undergoing – or maybe finally revealing – a process of orientalization, wishing to turn himself into a despot, an absolute monarch, like Alexander the Great, the Egyptian pharaohs or the Persian King of the Kings had been. This was utterly unacceptable for Roman citizens since nothing had been dearer to them than liberty from tyrannical rule since in 509 BC they had expelled their last Etruscan king Lucius Tarquinius Superbus from the city. This political union with the Queen of Egypt was a great threat to Rome and Romanitas, that is the very notion of being Roman, and certainly played a major role a few years later in the conspirators' decision to get rid of Caesar. Caesar arrived in Egypt in 48 BC and Caesarion (named after his father) was born in 47 BC, so dates would support the fact that Caesar really was his father. Cleopatra later associated him to her throne under the name of Ptolemy XV Caesar, but when Octavian won the civil war against Mark Antony and Egypt was conquered by the winning side, the boy was doomed. Antony and Cleopatra having committed suicide, Octavian most likely had him executed since he thought the presence of too many Caesars intolerable.

This strongly points to the fact that many thought and were convinced that Caesarion really was Caesar's natural son and to further prove paternity Hughes justly cites from Plutarch and Suetonius, in particular the following passage by the latter: 'Finally he [Caesar] called her [Cleopatra] to Rome and did not let her leave until he had ladened her with high honours and rich gifts, and he allowed her to give his name to the child which she bore. In fact, according to certain Greek writers, this child was very like Caesar in looks and carriage. Mark Antony declared to the senate that Caesar had really acknowledged the boy, and that Gaius Matius, Gaius Oppius, and other friends of Caesar knew this.'[12]

The evidence for Caesar's paternity seems incontrovertible. Gaius Oppius, Caesar's friend and the author on whose historical accounts later biographers would most likely rely, later produced a pamphlet in which he virulently denied the idea that Caesarion was Caesar's son. This was a political move to show his support for Octavian, Caesar's adopted son and the legitimate continuer of the Julian house. On account of this, as we examined Julia's case, we agree with Hughes on the importance of dissecting Caesarion's history looking for signs of epilepsy. Unfortunately no mention is ever made of such neurological problems in the young ruler of Egypt. Hughes, nonetheless, albeit acknowledging this limitation in the sources, quotes from two historical novels from 1973 and 2003 in which Caesarion is described as suffering from seizures of epileptic nature. This leads the scholar to affirm that 'Although historical novels, [...] both books emphasized Caesarion's inheritance of epilepsy from his father, Julius Caesar.' Commenting on this, we would strongly make the case against such untrustworthy sources being quoted in serious historical and medical dissertations, since they have no value and relevance whatsoever to the debate. Although the lack of primary sources as evidence is admitted and the reference to these novels is made as an example of how other writers have also speculated that Caesarion inherited epilepsy from his father, such references only generate confusion. By the same principle, were we to discuss examples of chastity and morality in the late Republican Roman elite, we should probably radically question Tacitus' statement about Atia Balba Caesonia, Augustus' mother, in his *Dialogue on the Orators*: 'In her presence it was the last offence to utter an unseemly word or to do a disgraceful act. With scrupulous piety and modesty she regulated not only the boy's studies and occupations, but even his recreations and games.'[13] Since in the greatly successful (and somewhat truculent) 2005 HBO series Atia – skilfully interpreted by the talented British actress Polly Walker – is portrayed – *absit iniuria verbis*! – as a lascivious and conspiratorial woman.[14] Or sticking to the topic of Caesar's children and their purported medical conditions, we could speculate that his fictional son Orgetorix – born of his union with Rhiannon, the fictional daughter of King Orgetorix of the Helvetii (first century BC, this one at least is real!), as created by the pen of the late and lamented Australian neurologist and superb novelist Dr Colleen McCullough (1937 – 2015), could also have experienced epileptic seizures in his childhood, thus providing further evidence for a family tree of epilepsy.[15] The number of possibilities at that point would only depend on the readers' imagination. The discussion about Caesar's health, instead, is a serious and difficult one and we will never stop stressing the importance to quote and carefully analyse only primary sources, leaving novels for idle Saturday afternoons.

Marcus Junius Brutus. He may hardly be included in the family tree since it has never been clarified whether he really was Caesar's son, although there is a possibility because of a well-known love affair between the general and his mother Servilia. Because of this, Kanngiesser opts for considering him too, simply to remark that Appian and Plutarch report optical hallucinations but, after making it clear that 'nothing [...] is known of Brutus suffering from any mental defect', he dismissed the eventuality of epileptic activity in his brain by endorsing a previous conclusion by Heinrich Schaefer, in that these hallucinations must have been 'a half-waking state caused by overwork.'[16]

Caligula. Hughes interprets the sudden faints and the inability to stand up or hold his head up as absence attacks, typical of childhood generalized epilepsy. To reinforce his diagnosis he also recalls the fact that he could not swim and considers the serious sufferings he had in 37 AD as a reference to encephalitis 'which' – Hughes writes – 'could have been a contributing factor to the bizarre features of his behaviour, which may well represent a temporal lobe syndrome'. This temporal lobe epilepsy, according to Hughes, could also explain his 'increased aggressiveness, emotionality, hypergraphia, altered sexual behaviour, increased hostility, manic tendencies, and anger and hostility'. Furthermore, the fact that he took pleasure in witnessing executions, indulged in violence for violence's sake, prostituted his sister and expressed several more signs of folly and delusional grandeur (he made his horse, Incitatus, a member of the senate and would claim to have had sex with the moon or mock the gods in public) could also be explained by his epilepsy, although, Hughes points out, 'the diagnosis of schizophrenia could also be considered'. In our opinion, Caligula's psychiatric and neurological problems are evident and their epileptic nature can certainly be counted a possibility. If he really developed it in his infancy, then we should speak of primary epilepsy. In any case, to say that he inherited it from Caesar and from his ancestors, including the one who died at Pisa, may indeed be going one step too far from what the evidence points to.

Britannicus. (41–55 AD). He was the son of Claudius and Messalina (17/20–48 AD) and a cousin of Caligula, killed by Nero who wanted to be the sole ruler of Rome. Hughes highlights the fact that Britannicus is said by Suetonius to have suffered from *morbus comitialis*. Since he died at 14, it is likely that in that case *morbus comitialis* really meant epilepsy, which, as underlined for Caligula, should have been primary epilepsy, as it appeared in childhood. Kanngiesser also focuses on Claudius's drunkenness affirming that 'it is a well-known fact that drunkards' children are often epileptic'.[17] With respect to this it would probably be more interesting to focus on Messalina's promiscuous sexual habits and her constant partaking in parties. Would she consume alcohol in great quantities during pregnancy thus paving the way for her son to develop some of the clinical conditions found in the foetal alcohol syndrome spectrum? We just do not know.

Summing up all this information, to make his case stronger Hughes finally addresses consanguinity within the Julio-Claudian house suggesting that this could have ensured 'a recessive mode of inheritance', adding some statistical calculations based on alleged epileptic manifestations through the whole family's sufficiently recorded generations:

'From Julius Caesar and his sister Julia, there were five generations to Caligula and Britannicus, involving eighteen individuals in the bloodstreams to each of them. The prevalence of seizures in this instance would be 3/18 (16.7 per cent). If the numbers are doubled to thirty-six to account for unknown brothers and sisters, the prevalence of the three with seizures would be 3/36 (8.3 per cent). The prevalence of epilepsy in those ancient days is unknown, but would not likely be as high as 8–17 per cent to account for these three individuals on a coincidental basis. Assuming the present prevalence rate of epilepsy as 0.4 per cent to apply to the Roman period, the epilepsy in these three Julio-Claudian members would be best explained on an inheritance, rather than coincidental, basis.'

And draws the conclusion that an inherited form of epilepsy can explain Julius Caesar's seizures.

As we have so far had the opportunity to explain, many members of this family tree cannot be regarded as epileptics with certainty. In some cases, for instance Caesarion, it is all about speculation and assumptions. In addition, this theory does not analyse the potential clinical presentations in women of the House, and does not pay attention to Augustus, Tiberius or Claudius. More information about Claudius will be given shortly as part of another proposed diagnosis featuring a genetically transmitted condition. More neurological data is highlighted in Kanngiesser's work, who describes the fourth Roman emperor as 'ruled by women, cruel' and, as we have already said, 'he drank'. Kanngiesser then cautiously hypothesizes that his 'peculiar gait', his dragging of his right leg and the fact that he 'shook his head constantly' could be explained by one of the following diagnoses: '*Tic convulsif? Tremor nervosus aut alcoholicus?*' that either by some habitual spasm or contraction of muscles in the face or extremities, or by a trembling originated by a neurological disease or alcoholic addiction. These hypotheses are of interest but do not describe Claudius, too, as an epileptic. In addition, as Benediktson wrote 'The epilepsies of Caligula and Britannicus both began in early life [...] and were genuine. Caligula's seizures abated after his teens, as is normal, and Britannicus' might also if he had lived longer. But Caesar's pathology is so different from theirs [ie Caligula's and Britannicus'] that it is difficult to agree with Esser that epilepsy was endemic to the Julian family. It could be Claudian or even Antonian, for Caligula and Britannicus were of all three families.'[18] We could not have put it better and in a clearer manner and we simply comment that, given the many branches of which the ruling house is composed, the description of an epileptic Julio-Claudian family tree is but an exercise in overstretching the literary sources.

Secondary Epilepsy
Several differential diagnoses have been suggested to explain the origin of the seizures: head trauma, syphilis, neurocystercosis, granulomatous infection, cardiovascular origin, brain tumour.

Note on Caesar's potential alcoholism

We have read in the biographies of the dictator that his diet was moderate and so was his consumption of alcohol. Nonetheless an episode in his life stands out which should be carefully examined and ruled out analytically since it raises the suspicion of alcoholism. It is difficult to exactly locate it chronologically, but we know that it happened at the prosecution of a head-to-head debate in the Senate House between Caesar and his political enemy and guardian of the traditional senatorial order Marcus Portius Cato Uticensis (95–46 BC). On that occasion (15 December 63 BC) the destiny of the arrested affiliates of traitor and public enemy Lucius Sergius Catilina (108–61 BC) was being debated and many senators were in favour of the death penalty. Nevetherless Caesar gave a speech against such a resolution, claiming that killing the men would have been against the institutions laid down by their ancestors. It comes as no surprise that Caesar's adversaries started claiming that he himself must have had some part in the conspiracy.

Something rather peculiar and slightly spicy ensues – let us follow Plutarch's accounts in his *Life of Cato Minor*:

> [...] 'on this occasion, when Caesar was eagerly engaged in a great struggle with Cato and the attention of the senate was fixed upon the two men, a little note was brought in from outside to Caesar. Cato tried to fix suspicion upon the matter and alleged that it had something to do with the conspiracy, and bade him read the writing aloud. Then Caesar handed the note to Cato, who stood near him. But when Cato had read the note, which was an unchaste letter from his sister Servilia to Caesar, with whom she was passionately and guiltily in love, he threw it to Caesar, saying, "Take it, thou sot," and then resumed his speech.'[19]

And in the *Life of Brutus*:

> 'It is said also that when the great conspiracy of Catiline, which came near overthrowing the city, had come to the ears of the senate, Cato and Caesar, who were of different opinions about the matter, were standing side by side, and just then a little note was handed to Caesar from outside, which he read quietly. But Cato cried out that Caesar was

outrageously receiving letters of instruction from the enemy. At this, a great tumult arose, and Caesar gave the missive, just as it was, to Cato. Cato found, when he read it, that it was a wanton bit of writing from his sister Servilia, and throwing it to Caesar with the words "Take it, thou sot," turned again to the business under discussion. So notorious was Servilia's passion for Caesar.'[20]

As underlined by Karl-Wilhelm Weeber,[21] even if wine was a much appreciated liquor in Roman society, we have extremely limited data on how widespread alcoholism might have been. We know that the Romans made a distinction between *ebrietas* (a state of transient drunkenness) and *ebriositas* (chronic drunkenness) and that, if there were proofs or gossip about somebody's alcoholic attitudes, this would be a likely political topic to be used in the fight for power against competitors. Is this also the case for Cato's words? Cato's rage must have been immense and the insult spat at his enemy and the seducer of his sister Servilia (mother of the famous Brutus) testifies to it. 'Sot' means 'drunkard' and is used in the English translation we chose, the Greek original being the vocative form μέθυσε *[méthyse]*. Μέθυσος [nominative, *méthysos*] is an adjective specifically meaning 'drunken with wine' and in a broader sense 'intemperate', in any case as a consequence of being drunk. Following Kanngiesser's note, we believe him to be largely correct when he writes that 'this remark only applies to Caesar's amorous disposition, which is well known through the writings of Catullus, Suetonius and Dio Cassius'.[22] In sum, he was drunk with love affairs and sexual intercourse, not with wine. The fact that, while he was no drunkard, Cato specifically chose to use such an insult strengthens the fact he must have been infuriated and that he opted for a completely false claim, or at least an out-of-context word, to heavily insult his opponent's dignity in public. Along the same lines, it has been highlighted in medical and classical literature that 'Caesar showed restraint when eating or drinking', thus trusting the general description of his habits found in the Plutarchean passage. As Hughes justly noted, alcoholism should not be considered on account of lack of evidence.

Head Trauma

Specific event/Military Likelihood – Variant

This stance has been voiced in recent times by the eminent Roman military historian Professor Barry Strauss (Cornell University, Ithaca, NY), who, commenting on our theory in Professor Kristina Killgrove's (University of West Florida) specialised bioarchaeology feature in *Forbes Magazine*, linked Plutarch's statement that Caesar first suffered from epilepsy in Corduba (Spain) 'which would suggest a specific event such as head trauma'.[23]

A few months after the debate in *Forbes*, taking our turn to comment, let us start by saying that head trauma can be caused by virtually anything but considering the general's hectic military activity in those years and his numerous exposures to trauma on the battlefield, it is sensible to think of such a trauma having occurred while on duty. This cause finds its foundations in Caesar's unrestrained warlike activity and in the fact that he would not simply direct the battle from a distance, like other more prudent commanders. Instead he would partake in the most life-risking situations. To testify this, it is said that after the Battle of Munda, which put an end to the Civil Wars (before they started again following Caesar's assassination in 44 BC), he asserted that, while upon several occasions he had fought for victory, that time he fought for life. He was a superb tactician but also a front line warrior whose capacity to motivate his men by his presence, strength, abnegation and courage allowed them to resist unbelievable toils in inhospitable foreign lands, far from home for many years. Because of this, it makes sense to think that he suffered injuries and that he might have received head traumas, which could have damaged the brain, thus paving the way for the development of epilepsy. This is seen even nowadays by neurologists who take care of patients treated after car accidents or even trauma occurring during sports competition.

This opinion is undoubtedly respectable, based on common sense knowledge of military engagement, therefore it should be included in the list of potential causes of Julius Caesar's alleged epilepsy. Nevertheless, issues arise when analysing the ancient sources since no mention is found of a major blow to his head or of any extraordinary traumatic event capable of putting his life and presence on the battlefield at stake. Considering almost every single and minute detail of Caesar's life has been reported, from his politics, love affairs, military decisions, grand strategy, conspiracies, early life events, and countless anecdotes, it appears a little unlikely that a major trauma was not, even briefly and vaguely, reported in the ancient sources. One may be of the opinion that he deliberately chose to conceal this and that his men respected his will in order not to make him appear any weaker in the eyes of his enemies. In truth, could this have happened in Roman Spain, where the two rival armies of Pompey's deputies and his own were fighting? Is it possible that nobody, absolutely nobody from the enemy camp, noticed and reported so serious an injury and spread the news, even making it bigger and more sensational than it was, to vanquish Caesar's propaganda machine, depicting him for the first time as an old wounded beast, ready to be killed? Such being the case, could it be that such an injury occurred in Gaul, where his troops were the only Roman presence and where the Gauls may not have been able to take proper advantage of this potential accident from a political and military point of view? Hypothetically, another possibility would be that there was no one big blow, but that several minor or medium traumas produced a cumulative effective. This would explain the absence of any reference to a major trauma in the sources.

On the one hand, this hypothesis, which is historiographically relevant and goes beyond the boundaries of an epilepsy-yes-or-no discussion – no matter its outcomes, whether it really be epilepsy or other clinical problems of a different nature – deserves the utmost respect and will not be discarded hastily and *a priori*. On the other hand, like other authors,[24] we still stress the fact that more primary evidence of a major traumatic event in the Greco-Roman sources would be necessary for us to be persuaded by it, in lieu of other etiologies.

Literary-Sculptural Evidence – Variant

In the opening paragraphs of our book we have touched upon the fact artistic representations of Caesar's morphology can only offer us a vague and uncertain perception of what he looked like. Similarly, we cannot expect those statues or minted coins to give any vital detail on his health. Nonetheless, a certain 'school of thought' believes the evidence for his head trauma can be identified. We used inverted commas for such orientation, since there does not seem to be any particular author who has fully formulated or embraced it and its consequence, while there are but scarce hints in medical literature, pretty much side considerations to enrich the (already crowded) range of differential diagnoses.

Gomez and colleagues,[25] for instance, discuss the passage in Suetonius where the Roman author reports how it was customary (*semel in anno*, we should say, if not in a lifetime!) during the triumph parade through Rome for Caesar's soldiers to make fun of their general by calling him *moechus calvus*, adulterous bald man. Precisely they would sing '*Urbani, servate uxores; moechum calvum adducimus: / Aurum in Gallia effutuisti, hic sumpsisti mutuum*', which in polite English could be translated into something like 'Citizens, watch your wives; we bring a bald adulterer: in Gaul you spent on prostitutes the money, that you borrowed here.'[26] As we said, this is a polished version of what ought to be translated in a more colourful manner, which we leave to the readers' imagination. While it can be doubted that Caesar took personal offence for the first part (even if loudly remarked in public) since he was well known to have always been an insatiable *tombeur de femmes*, we know that the second part caused him great shame and resentment, to the extent that the idea of some consequent psychological impairment or discomfort could even be cautiously considered. Suetonius' description later goes on to say: 'He was somewhat overnice in the care of his person, being not only carefully trimmed and shaved, but even having superfluous hair plucked out, as some have charged; while his baldness was a disfigurement the would have troubled him greatly, since he found that it was often the subject of the gibes of his detractors.'[27] The Latin has the phrase '*calvitii vero deformitatem iniquissime ferret*'. The authors' endeavour to elaborate the word *deformitas* trying to understand if this 'disfigurement' or 'deformity' really was a genuine cranial deformity or if it simply meant an 'absence of beauty' but they simply offer the double possibility without drawing any conclusions.

The authors also note that 'although no skull deformities were seen, it is interesting to note that in all coinage Caesar appears with a wreath, whereas in all busts and statues his head is uncovered.' Which is interesting artistically but does not add anything relevant to our discourse.

Professor Fabrizio Bruschi (University of Pisa), analyzing Caesar's health and old hypotheses, gives some more information since he affirms that 'the head asymmetry in the Tusculum portrait, possibly the only surviving bust of Caesar made during his lifetime, has been interpreted as evidence of trauma that occurred early in his life'.[28] Pathological connotations were first suggested for this admirable portrait in a 1943 study by Maurizio Borda. The author writes:[29] 'The irregular shape of the head with its abnormal left-side development, the only asymmetric element in this head which is all symmetries, is eye-catching.' He also specifies: 'The head, of a rather elongated and salient shape, somewhat developed in the occiput, shows two interesting pathological deformations: its superior part, at the point called 'bregma', is depressed as if it were a saddle (a phenomenon called by physiologists 'clinocephaly'); while there is evident, in the front view, an excessive development of the left parietal region ('plagiocephaly'). This asymmetry is found in other portraits of Caesar;' and quoting from another book he expands his description: 'Observing Caesar's head in the most well-known statues, it appears evident how the left half of the skull cap, and actually the temporo-parietal region on the same side, is more prominent. If this were true, that is if this asymmetry matched a physiognomic and organic objective sign in the living person, it would have great significance, since it would certify an excess development of the area of the left cerebral hemisphere, in the section destined to the centre for the production of articulated speech and in general body movements.' Strictly anatomically speaking, these two observations, plagiocephaly and clinocephaly, seem to be incontestable. They are the result of specific cases of craniosynostosis, a condition occurring in new-borns when cranial bones are still malleable, in which premature ossification of cranial sutures (the border between the bones of the skull) accounts for diminished development in one region: since the skull is unable to expand perpendicular to the sutures that underwent fusion, it grows parallel to the fused sutures. This process affects the overall morphology of the head and if this compensatory growth does not furnish enough space for proper brain development, impairment of mental health and other neurological issues are a possible outcome. More interesting information can be found in Flemming S Johansen's analysis of the bust: 'The portrait is dolichocephalic and the forehead is strongly arched as on woman.

This kind of abnormality in a skull is of no interest from a pathological point of view. It exists all over the world in all races and is without any medical importance for the individual who has this abnormality.'[30]

These notes about the Tusculum cranium are very interesting and the following considerations may be made: firstly, the possibility that the head shows the result of a head trauma should be ruled out since, if they really existed in the living subject, such deformations almost certainly developed when Caesar was in his infancy; secondly, their influence on his mental faculties should not be exaggerated, or even considered at all, both in terms of an expansion of them in the overly developed left half of the skull, and in terms of pathological infirmity since we know that throughout his life his cognitive functions were remarkable; thirdly, since these deformities must have developed as he was passing through his mother's uterus or during his first months of life and might have been caused by several factors (including biomechanical, environmental, genetic and hormonal ones), if one insists on thinking that he was epileptic already as a child or very young adult, one should identify this head reshaping as the ultimate causative factor. If that be the case, then one would have to explain why no reference at all to epileptic fits is given in accounts of his early life, why Suetonius clearly states that his health problems (including the alleged *morbus comitialis*) began towards the end of his life and finally why no sign of mental and cognitive retardation has ever been reported when describing his first years. In fact, even if such a deformation really caused epileptic seizures, it is very hard to believe that these would have been the sole pathological manifestation, since the whole brain would have been affected. From this we conclude that, the Tusculum bust being a veritable depiction of Caesar's head morphology towards the end of his life, we must be of the opinion that clinocephaly and plagiocephaly characterised him, that he probably developed them as a new-born but also that they did not cause him to develop any neurological problem at all, let alone epilepsy. Persevering in historical discussions with the myth of the Tusculum bust being the tangible proof of Caesar suffering from head trauma or developing superhuman faculties or even the ill-famed epilepsy in childhood, is indeed an idle sport, uncorroborated by evidence, logic or even common sense. If the head trauma hypothesis is to be maintained, then Barry Strauss's view is the sole historically sensible one.

Syphilis

The possibility that Caesar suffered from a sexually transmitted disease (STD) must certainly be investigated on the grounds of his almost mythological love affairs and famed sex life about which Suetonius annotates: 'But to remove all doubt that he had an evil reputation both for shameless vice and for adultery, I have only to add that the elder Curio in one of his speeches calls him "every woman's man and every man's woman".'[31]

Speaking of orientation, it is not doubted that Caesar had bisexual experiences, since, while he was primarily interested in enjoying the pleasures of women's company, he conceded himself to having sex with at least two men, one being king Nicomedes of Bythinia, the latter being Mamurra (first century BC), a military officer who served Caesar during the Gallic wars and probably also during the civil wars. As we saw, he allegedly slept with Nicomedes when he was only 19 years old, resulting in the mocking epithet of 'Queen of Bythinia'. This caused him great outrage and would probably have provoked his alpha-male side, leading him to want to seduce as many women as possible, to compensate for the mark the vile jokes and heavy attacks had left on his reputation. The problem with his relationship with Nicomedes was not necessarily homosexuality, which to a certain extent was tolerated in ancient Rome, but the fact that he had allegedly been passive during the act, thus he had been subdued by the Asian king. While a woman behaves so for anatomical reasons, he – his fellow Romans believed – should have subdued Nicomedes, but by choosing, or allowing himself, to be penetrated he behaved in too feminine a way to be acceptable to the virile Roman standards and mindsets. The famous poet Gaius Valerius Catullus (84 – 54 BC) was never very kind when talking about Caesar and in one of his poems (*Carmen 93*) he made it perfectly clear that he did not care at all about Caesar and his power: 'I am not over anxious, Caesar, to please you greatly, or to know whether you are a white or a black man.'[32]

It is then no astonishment that he cashed in on the rumours (or even direct evidence) that Caesar and Mamurra were enjoying themselves intimately and he left us two spicy and somewhat vulgar pieces of poetry denigrating Mamurra's service in Gaul and explaining the nature of his 'friendship' with Caesar. They are so direct and plain that it makes no sense to comment upon them, hence we simply quote so readers' can understand the details.

In *Carmen 29* Catullus most kindly addresses Mamurra as 'mentula', a more colourful variant of the generally used word for the male anatomical member:

'Who can see this, who can stand it, save the shameless, the glutton, and gambler that Mamurra Mentula should possess what long-haired Gaul had and remotest Britain had before? You sodomite Romulus, will you see this and bear it? Then you are shameless, a glutton and a gambler. And will he now, proud and overflowing, saunter over each one's bed, like a little white dove or an Adonis? You sodomite Romulus, will you see this and bear it? Then you are shameless, a glutton and a gambler. For such a name, Generalissimo, have you been to the furthest island of the west, that this love-weary Mentula of yours should squander twenty or thirty million? What is it but a skewed liberality? Perhaps he spent too little, or perhaps he was washed clean? First he wasted his patrimony; second the loot from Pontus; then third the loot from Spain, which even the gold bearing Tagus knows. Now he is feared by Gauls and Britain. Why do you indulge this scoundrel? What can he do but devour well-fattened inheritances? Was it for such a name, † most wealthy father-in-law and son-in-law, that you have destroyed everything?'[33]

In *Carmen 57* he describes Caesar and Mamurra as two degenerates who share the same women and indulge in a disgusting sexual affair, and also confirms Caesar's bisexual orientation:

'Beautifully it fits the shameless sodomites, Mamurra and sexually submissive Caesar. It's no wonder: they share like stains—the one from the City, the other, Formian—which stay deep-marked and they cannot be washed off. Debauched twins each, both learned, both in one bed, one not more than the other the greater greedier adulterer, allied rivals of the girls. Beautifully it fits the shameless sodomites.'[34]

From these poems it is indeed very hard to ascertain whether Caesar engaged Mamurra in a manlier manner, according to Roman standards, than he reportedly failed to with Nicomedes but the references to their being rivals and mates in their quest for girls, seems to describe both of them as womanisers. No more information can be drawn from later poems, since, as Suetonius recounts, Catullus and Caesar made peace.

Speaking of heterosexual relationships, Caesar had countless sexual escapades[35] with women of whom we mention four individuals who are also recorded by Gomez and colleagues. These are his three successive wives Cornelia, Pompeia, Calpurnia; Cleopatra, the Queen of Egypt; Eunoë, the wife of Bogudes, King of Mauretania; Pompey's and Crassus's wives; Servilia, Brutus' mother, and so forth. To these a certain number of prostitutes or occasional lovers history has forgotten to mention should perhaps be added to the list. A passage from Dio Cassius, where a series of extravagant honours and flatteries directed at him by adulators to please his ego is listed, testifies that until the end of his life he was extremely sexually active:

'When they had begun to honour him, it was with the idea, of course, that he would be reasonable; but as they went on and saw that he was delighted with what they voted – indeed he accepted all but a very few of their decrees – different men at different times kept proposing various extravagant honours, some in a spirit of exaggerated flattery and others by way of ridicule. At any rate, some actually ventured to suggest permitting him to have intercourse with as many women as he pleased, because even at this time, though fifty years old, he still had numerous mistresses.'[36]

Because of this irrepressible sexual activity, a few common sexually transmitted diseases should be considered differentially. This was first done by Professor Michael Rieder[37] (University of Western Ontario), who focused on herpes, gonorrhoea, and chlamydia:

i. & ii. Herpes and gonorrhoea should be excluded since they would leave physical marks on Caesar's body and we would expect somebody to have noticed and reported it. These two conditions, we like to add, would not have caused epilepsy anyhow, since neurological complications of genital herpes are extremely rare and would be limited to involvement of the sacral segment of the spinal cord resulting in pain and paraesthesia but nothing at all like seizures, while in the case of untreated gonorrhoea meningitis is a likely eventuality and seizures would be a fairly commonly associated clinical sign, but meningitis would not comply with the description that Caesar was generally in good health and certainly not in a life-threatening situation of acute brain inflammation;

iii. Chlamydia (infection caused by *Chlamydia trachomatis*) should also be excluded since the clinical picture is much less incapacitating in men than it is in women. It becomes a more serious problem in men if prostatitis (inflammation of the prostate gland) is developed, but this would not limit somebody's quality of life or his ability to live an active life immersed in society and business too much. In addition, chlamydia would not cause such prominent neurological symptoms as those specifically attributed to Caesar.

Syphilis is a clinical possibility that we are left with although its historical origins and presentations remain controversial. Its existence in Roman Europe, however, is currently considered by many to be unlikely. The French doctor Donnadieu, discussing the possibility that his alleged epilepsy came from his sexual exploits, once famously wrote '*Il aimait les femmes, toutes les femmes, disaient ses soldats; on conviendra que ce n'est pas un signe d'epilepsie: il y aurait bien des épileptiques par le monde!*', 'He loved women, all the women, his soldiers said; one will concur that this is not a sign of epilepsy: there would be many epileptics around the world!'.[38] Despite this remark, a mix of humour and common sense, the possibility of syphilis should be examined before being ruled out as amongst its complications, as we will explain in a moment, there can even be epilepsy. This disease is a chronic condition that can be subdivided into three main phases following contagion through genital *mucosae*:

a. primary syphilis: a firm painless skin ulceration which classically evolves from a macule to a papule and finally to an erosion or ulcer;
b. secondary syphilis : after 2-4 months a rash develops and several mucosal lesions as well as several organs are involved;
c. tertiary syphilis : after a long asymptomatic phase which can last up to several years, major systems such as the cardiovascular and the nervous

can become affected, the former by aorta aneurysm, the latter by *tabes dorsalis* (or syphilitic myelopathy) a slow degeneration of the nerves in the spinal cord. In the last eventuality the key lesion is known as *gumma*, namely a focus of granulomatous inflammation, not dissimilar in appearance from tubercular granuloma, which eventually degrades via liquefactive necrosis, resulting in deforming scars. In the context of neurosyphilis epileptic seizures are a fairly common find.

Historically known under several different names such as French or Neapolitan disease, this condition plagued Europe for centuries, nevertheless when it first made its appearance in the old world is still disputed. While there is evidence for its presence in the Americas before Columbus (1450/1451 – 1506), a heated debated has been going on over whether it was also already present in Europe. On the basis of this two hypotheses[39] dominate the controversy:

a. Syphilis did not exist in Europe until the Conquistadores brought it back home with them.
b. Syphilis has already existed for a long time but it was only paid proper attention and fully clinically described after Columbus' voyages.

Over the last few years a series of studies conducted on skeletal remains have questioned the assumption that syphilis was brought to Europe from the Americas. The most recent of these studies, published in the *Anthropologischer Anzeiger*,[40] focused on skeletal remains found at an archaeological site in Austria dated back to pre-Columbian times. Dental analysis showed lesions which the researchers interpret as signs of syphilis. The skeleton belonging to a sub-adult, the specific case of syphilis would be one of congenital syphilis that is a condition passed on from mother to foetus. Focusing on Roman times, Dr Penso, making excellent use of literary evidence from the encyclopaedists Celsus and Plinius, as well as the poets Horace (65–27 BC) and Martial (38/41–102/104 AD), highlights the possibility of lesions of the genitalia called '*indurate*' or even '*condylomata*', which today would point to syphilis. He also highlights how ancient Romans did not often allow doctors to treat their lesions, since they were ashamed of them.[41] In spite of this, while new anthropological studies may offer fresh insights into the possibility of Pre-Columbian existence of syphilis in Europe and ancient literary sources may suggest the presence of the disease, caution should be the rule, especially when conclusions are drawn from a single skeleton or vague references in old texts. In addition, as far as skeletal changes are concerned, those produced by syphilis can also be caused by other diseases, they are not specific only to syphilis. In sum, the question remains a great dilemma but the post-Columbian hypothesis seems to be holding ground. In this case, we exclude the possibility that Caesar had seizures caused by tertiary syphilis.

Vascular Disease

Arteriosclerosis

This cause was briefly proposed by Dr Kanngiesser in 1932[42] who suggested that it might have provoked what once used to be called *epilepsia tarda*. This definition, meaning 'late or senile epilepsy', is a somewhat archaic name for late onset epilepsy and it was fairly common in the last century, which, for clarity's sake, ought to be explained. An article that appeared in 1927 in the *Annals of Internal Medicine* verified that a great confusion existed concerning the exact meaning. Some authors would restrict it to those cases of 'idiopathic epilepsy' of later life which present no evidence of cerebral arteriosclerosis or other organic disease. Others on the contrary – and this includes most of the modern writers – feel that senile epilepsy is in some way related to disturbances of the cerebral circulation incident to cerebral arterioclerosis and atheroma.[43] The latter seems to be the way in which Kanngiesser used the term. The 1927 article, now showing the author's interpretation, also adds: 'we would label with the term *epilepsia tarda* those patients who exhibit recurrent generalised epileptiform seizures after 40 years of age and who fail to show any sufficient etiologic factor other than a background of circulatory inadequacy, with special reference to periodic insufficiency of the cerebral circulation.' This adds further clarification to the rather vague definition of *epilepsia tarda*, even if at the same time it brings some extra confusion since generalized seizures are normally idiopathic (genetic). In any case, as we have explained above, it may well be that crisis focal at onset may develop into generalized ones (thus involving the two hemispheres of the brain) as a second step.

The reference to 'circulatory inadequacy' is indeed very interesting and relevant to our personal view of the facts: we shall see in the following chapters how similar ideas grounded in this clinical rationale have produced some conciliatory responses to our investigation even in those who still stick to the *epileptic non plus ultra*.

Going back to Kanngiesser's theory with a (hopefully) clearer understanding of *epilepsia tarda*, as we briefly touched upon, he was the first to link Caesar's father's death to his son's disease, thus providing some reason for a full clinical interpretation in the light of cardiovascular pathology. Moreover, he calls the sudden death of Julius Caesar senior 'apoplexy'. As in the case of *epilepsia tarda*, apoplexy is an outdated definition. In the past, more or less until the beginning of the twentieth century and to a certain extent in loose and imprecise medical talk, this term was used to classify symptoms such as sudden losses of consciousness leading to death, their actual causes potentially being all major cardiovascular problems, such as strokes, myocardial infarction or rupture of aneurisms (ie a dilation, a bulge) of the aorta. Giuseppe Penso[44] notes how Pliny uses the word *ictus* (stroke) in the same sense used by the Greek medical author Arateus of Cappadocia (probably first century AD) when referring to paralysis-causing apoplexy, that is the complete deprivation of movement, sensibility and consciousness. For this reason, it is difficult to translate it absolutely correctly but certainly one of the proposed sudden life-threatening or death-causing cardiovascular events would undoubtedly fit and, focusing specifically on the symptoms, would confirm what our philological reflections on the word *exanimatus* evoked.

Now, in detail, what is arteriosclerosis and how could this have caused Caesar's epilepsy within the clinical background furnished by Kanngiesser? Arteriosclerosis is a disease of the arteries consisting of degenerative processes such as thickening, hardening and grave loss of elasticity of the walls of the arteries. If the arteries can no longer expand and contract rhythmically as they should in normal circulation, blood supply to the organs becomes impaired, with a list of bad consequences for the body. If the organ that suffers most from this shortage of supply is the brain, then it is very easy to understand that the main functions of human life such as attention, communication, vision, processing of information, even consciousness and balance are endangered. In addition, such cardiovascular impairments to the brain may also be responsible for the genesis of epilepsy. Given Caesar's advanced (if not already old) age at the time of the first episodes of his disease, this theory deserves great respect and we will have time to expand on it, yet it should be stressed that its major limitations are basically the fact that Kanngiesser did not pay, in our opinion, enough attention to the other case of 'apoplexy' mentioned in the famous Plinian passage, hence failing to fully understand and elaborate a retrospective genetic background of cardiovascular disease in Julius's family. Furthermore, Hughes correctly points out that 'there is no evidence that Caesar's remarkable cognitive faculties has diminished in any way toward the end of his life, as one would expect in advancing arteriosclerosis'.[45] This limits the possibilities of atherosclerosis as the specific cause, yet, as it will be explained, other cardiovascular etiologies may well be considered. In sum, Kanngiesser's theory has several merits and of the many commentators who have succeeded him he was probably the sole one to come close to the truth, or at least the most plausible answer to Caesar's ailments.

Arteriovenous malformation

As the term suggests, arteriovenous malformation (AVM) is an abnormal connection between two different types of blood vessels, arteries and veins. As we all know, arteries bring oxygenated and nutrients-rich blood to peripheral tissues and organs, while veins remove deoxygenated blood and what remains of those nutrients after biochemical transformation within cells (catabolites). In normal anatomy, the meeting point is a fine net of connections provided by small thin vessels called capillaries. If this capillary connection is bypassed and a direct communication between arteries and veins exists, then we exactly have arteriovenous malformations. Such an anomaly can exist everywhere in the body, but the most well-known occurrences are the cerebral ones.

The theory was first considered by Gomez and colleagues in 1995 among the sensible differential diagnoses:

'The possibility of arteriovenous malformation in one of the cerebral hemispheres should be considered in a patient with convulsions and headache. These lesions are composed of an abnormal tangle of vessels which may rupture and produce the picture of subarachnoid haemorrhage, a serious condition which probably would have been recognized by his contemporaries. In addition, this congenital malformation usually manifest themselves at an early age.'[46]

On account of the absence of early age presentation and of low likelihood of a subarachnoid haemorrhage which his contemporaries would have noted since it would have caused him to suffer a major blow, although from inside his skull, to a certain extent as if he had suffered from head trauma. Nevertheless, just a few weeks after the publication of our study in *Neurological Sciences*, Montemurro and colleagues published a new hypothesis[47] built on the finally justly estimated cardiovascular background in the Julian family. The authors affirm: 'In our opinion, although it is not possible to state for sure that Julius Caesar had a brain arteriovenous malformation (AVM), we cannot exclude it. A brain AVM can explain both seizures and all other symptoms related to a cerebrovascular pathology.' They subsequently note that 'although patients with AVM often have their first seizures before the age of 50, a number of patients suffer their first haemorrhage in advanced years.' Having explained the background and limitations, they summarise Caesar's psychological symptoms, namely 'altered mental status, personality changes, and/or new neurologic deficits' and motor symptoms 'vertigo, sensory deficit, limb paresis and gait disturbances', asserting that all these could be explained in terms of AVM. In particular the last group would be the result of 'a common AVM steal phenomenon', which means that blood volume and rate are not evenly distributed and certain areas may receive more supply than neighbouring ones. Furthermore, the authors are of the opinion that headaches, which we saw to have been also reported for Caesar, may be a fairly common presentation in AVM patients. To support this they quote from two recent clinical studies showing 'headache as first clinical presentation in 12.6 per cent and 13 per cent of their patients, respectively'.

Given this hypothesis is rooted in the cardiovascular field and tightly linked to our own, both chronologically and as far as the core argument is concerned, we will comment more on it in chapter four when our stance will be explained at length. For now suffice it to say that this diagnosis is interesting but is weakened by the two elements underlined in the 1995 article: AVM typically manifest at an early age and a rupture would have been recognised by contemporaries. The authors fail to address these major points and simply strengthen their stance by means of the fact that some AVM patients experience their first clinical manifestations in late life.

This hypothesis has several merits but it patently struggles to preserve epilepsy at any cost and the impression is that the historico-philological tools are loosely implemented throughout the investigation. The excellent bibliography and clear display of the key pathological facts in Caesar's life, without forgetting the already mentioned reference to the doctor staying with the young Julius on the pirates' island, certainly make this work relevant and way more than some historical vignette. For this reason it should be included in the select book list of serious historical monographs. Nonetheless, the conclusions drawn in the paper, albeit much sounder than other proposed etiologies, are very charming, but slightly stale buns.

Granulomatous Infections

These represent a varied group of diseases with specific clinical presentations that have in common the formation of granulomas, pathological formations described as compact grouping of inflammatory cells with predominance of mononuclear cells, which assemble as a result of the persistent presence of non-degradable products or as a consequence of a hypersensitivity response. Probably the most well-known member of this group is tuberculosis (TB), in the past called phthisis, a widespread infectious disease caused by *Mycobacterium tuberculosis*. When the disease affects the brain, the chances that epilepsy, as well as other neurological signs, could develop increase considerably. Tuberculosis was very widespread in the past and certainly Caesar could have caught it during his travels, but, as McLachlan correctly points out, epileptic seizures would have been 'in association with other signs of encephalopathy', while there is no such indication that can possibly be derived from the ancient accounts of his life.[48]

Neurocysticercosis

The clinical possibility of neurocysticercosis was first summarily considered and basically ruled out on the basis of lack of information by Gomez and colleagues in 1995,[49] who wrote: 'Did the Roman emperor have a parasitosis of the brain? Cysticercosis, hydatidosis and other types of parasites invade the brain and produce headaches and convulsions. No information is available other than symptoms suggesting the patient had malaria in his youth. Parasitic infections are common in areas of low hygienic care where food and water may be contaminated.' Despite this, the hypothesis was resumed and expounded at length by Dr Richard S McLachlan in a 2010 historical review featuring in *The Canadian Journal of Neurological Sciences*.[50]

Cystercosis is parasitic infection contracted from poorly cooked pork containing the larval stage of the tapeworm *Taenia solium*. Pigs are the intermediate host swallowing the eggs from the environment: the eggs then open in the swine intestine and the parasites, making their way through the intestinal wall, reach the bloodstream and colonise striate muscles where the larvae become cysts, called cysticercus. In the adult form the worm can become 6 to 12 metres long and stay in the human intestine for up to 25 years, leaving the patient almost asymptomatic, other than occasional dyspepsia (ie difficult digestion) and abdominal pain. When cysts are formed in the brain, neurocysticercosis ensues and epilepsy is one, if not the only, clinical manifestation. McLachlan believes that Julius Caesar was infected by this tapeworm during his campaigns in North Africa, thus either in Egypt (48 BC) or Tunisia (46 BC).

Integrating his reflections with some historical background, we would like to underline that such worms were known to the ancients and the very word *taenia* was used by the often cited Pliny, even if he appears to distinguish properly between tapeworms and roundworms, since he happens to mention *tineae* (a spelling alternative) *rotunda* (ie round tapeworms). Other authors mention several type of worms and seem to be well acquainted with the symptoms caused by parasitic infection and also, very interestingly, appear to testify to the presence of effective remedies against them. While there is little doubt about these allusions to worms and their ability to colonise and affect the intestine, it is pure speculation to say whether they were able to link neurological signs such as focal epilepsy with a spread of the infection to brain tissue.[51]

Commenting on it one year later, Fabrizio Bruschi remarked: 'The hypothesis of neurocysticercosis is undoubtedly intriguing, but it is based on exclusion criteria. Unfortunately, it is impossible to perform neuroimaging analysis or serological tests on Caesar to have a confirmation of such a diagnosis.'[52] The theory had a big impact at the time and was even touched upon in the episode of the History Channel series *Ancients Behaving Badly*, covering the psychological profiling, disease and deeds of Julius Caesar. McLachlan's proposition was put forward at the end of a very productive septenate in which, going from 2003 until 2010, multidisciplinary approaches and advanced state-of-the-art techniques were implemented to reinterpret Caesar's history, after critically re-examining the scant and rather ambiguous evidence provided by the ancient sources. Although not always necessarily stated in clear terms, until then three ideas were accepted as common sense and had *de facto* reigned supreme in Caesarian scholarship for quite a long time:

i.   That the Julio-Claudian house had been a compactly ill family tree in which inherited neuropsychiatric traits such as madness could be easily traced from Julius Caesar down to Nero.
ii. That until the end of his life Caesar was in perfectly good shape and that psychological changes were only histrionic attempts to check people's reaction to his growing quasi-monarchical power or to upset the old senatorial class onto which he had imposed the yoke of servitude.
iii. As a follow up to ii, that his apparently changed behaviour had no part whatsoever in the final days of his life, in his last decisions and acts and in the conspirators' reaction to this, as well as their timing and planning.
iv. That the conspiracy to assassinate him was something of which Caesar was totally unaware.

The outcomes of these several new studies have been fairly positive in that new light has been shed on the last days of Caesar's life, offering novel and powerful insights into his final decline, but also a little negative on account of much too hurried conclusions being drawn about certain points, as we shall see in Chapter Five, and also of the failure to produce a uniform and scholarly written theory capable of coherently and exhaustively explaining his disease and the role it played in his ultimate demise. The rather showy televised form in which certain ideas were presented in that period have had a tremendous impact on the perception of Julius Caesar's disease and the last months of his life, yet they have erected a wall separating these fresh new ideas from the world of traditional classical scholarship. In sum, they have flourished in clinical debates and have captivated people's minds but have failed to be organically discussed by professional Caesarian scholars. This book humbly tries to heal the wound, opening a gap in that impenetrable academic barricade. Specifically focusing on McLachlan's hypothesis, this certainly has a fascination and because of its superb mixture of neurological theory with anthropological information about consumption of pork meat in North Africa and the Middle East in the ancient world and with hard evidence from a palaeopathological study on an Egyptian mummy it surely deserves respect.[53] In our opinion, this stance basically suffers from three major weaknesses:

a. It does not satisfactorily answer – even speculatively – the difficulty highlighted in the 1995 work, namely that no information about infectious disease or parasitic infections, other than malaria in his youth, is ever mentioned in the sources;

b. It points specifically to *Taenia solium* as the causative agent of Caesar's epilepsy, when other types of worms could also be involved in the cerebral pathology. In particular, *T. multiceps* could be responsible for very similar cerebral manifestation as *T. solium* already in the larval stage, a condition called coenuruses. A much rarer possibility would be the hydatidosis mentioned in 1995. This condition is named after hydatid cysts, formation enclosing another parasite *Echinococcus Granulosus*, for which dogs are the definitive host, while other humans, ovines and pigs can be intermediate hosts. Its pathologic outcomes are explained in terms of a mass effect on the invaded organ; if it is the brain, then focal neurological signs are to be expected. Against this last possibility in Caesar's case, we could say that the effects of an infection by *Echinococcus Granulosus* tend to be seen rather early, while, even according to McLachlan's reconstruction of the facts, he must have been asymptomatic for a couple of years following infection in Africa;

c. It shows one major chronological issue. Let's focus on this passage from the author's work: '[...] the best documented of Caesar's seizures was at Thapsus in 46 BC about a year after he first travelled to Egypt. This would be consistent with the slow progression of the disease if he acquired it in North Africa. Plutarch states that he had another seizure in Cordoba in Spain where he led his troops shortly after Thapsus. However he was also in that city three years earlier as governor so which of these two visits Plutarch is referring to is unclear. It is likely the second visit as it would be unusual for someone with late onset untreated epilepsy from any cause to go three years before a second convulsion occurred.' McLachlan accepts Thapsus (46 BC) as an episode of epilepsy and is of the opinion that the Corduba one mentioned by Plutarch must have occurred in 45 BC, that is after Thapsus. The sequence would be coherent with Suetonius's statement that his disease started at the end of his life and it would mean that Caesar was presumably infected by the tapeworm in North Africa, so either in 48 BC when he was in Egypt with Cleopatra or exactly in 46 BC when he was fighting Labienus and Cato the Younger and when the Thapsus incident took place. What is not convincing in this hypothesis is the translation, rather interpretation, the author gives for Plutarch's reference to Corduba. McLachlan writes 'another seizure', while we have already seen that the Greek author specifically says that these epileptic fits were 'a trouble which first attacked him, we are told, in Corduba.' This, as we explained in depth, means that it must have happened anytime (most likely 49 BC) before, not after, his campaigns in North Africa (48 BC and 46 BC). Such being the case, one is left with two eventualities:

i. Plutarch is not reliable, thus, even if he says that they occurred there for the first time, it may well be that the fits presented after Caesar had been in Africa. If that is the case, how could one then believe the Thapsus episode to be hard evidence of seizures? Could it not be that Plutarch was referring to something else or had confused it with another occurrence?

ii. Plutarch has it right when he writes that the first fits happened in
Corduba, for this reason Caesar developed them before his travels to
North Africa, where this hypothesis posits his infection took place.

Despite being inclined towards the idea that Caesar was infected in Africa
and that the Corduba reference must be thought of as 45 BC, McLachlan also
briefly touched upon the other possibility:

'If it [ie 49 BC] is the first visit, then Caesar would have to have been
exposed to the disease during his extensive travels in southern Europe
since he had not yet been to Africa.'

This is indeed possible but he had been travelling extensively to Southern
Europe even in his youth and, as underlined by Gomez and colleagues, no
information whatsoever is found in the sources. So would this infection
have happened, for instance, during the hard-fought campaign in mainland
Greece (48 BC) against the Republican army? It is obviously a possibility, but
we know that, during the Greek campaign of the Civil War that followed his
victories in Italy and Spain, when Caesar's army was fighting Pompey's army
at Dyrrachium (modern day Durrës, or Durazzo, Albania), the situation
was not rosy, both in terms of military accomplishments and of supplies. He
would in fact soon thereafter be defeated by Pompey and forced to retreat
to regroup and motivate his men again. Pompey would fail fully to cash in
on the military advantage and give Caesar, a wounded but not yet killed lion
another chance and this would prove a fatal mistake. In his *Commentaries on the
Civil War*, talking in the third person as was his custom, Caesar gives us some
fundamental first-hand information about the hardships in that juncture:

'But Caesar, with an inferior force, besieged Pompey, whose troops were
entire, in good order, and abounded in all things [...] whereas Caesar's
army, having consumed all the corn round about, was reduced to the
last necessities. Nevertheless the soldiers bore all with singular patience;
remembering that though reduced to the like extremity the year before,
in Spain, they had yet, by their assiduity and perseverance, put an end
to a very formidable war [...] When barley or pulse was given them

instead of corn, they took it cheerfully; and thought themselves regaled when they got any cattle, which Epirus furnished them with in great abundance. They discovered in the country a root, called **chara**, which they pounded and kneaded with milk, so as to make a sort of bread of it. This furnished a plentiful supply; and when their adversaries reproached them with their want, by way of answer to their insults, they threw their loaves at them. By this time, the corn began to ripen, and the hopes of a speedy supply supported the soldiers under their present wants.'[54]

We know that Caesar, in a propaganda move or simply to extol his merits in the face of a magnified enemy, could have exaggerated the situation on certain occasions. In this case, however, the situation was really getting worse. Courage and will to fight and win were no doubt more abundant items than food supplies. At Dyrrachium and during the regrouping Caesar's soldiers, as he writes, had been through so many hardships in the past that they were not scared and prepared to suffer. Why would they do so? Because he shared with them exactly those very hardships they were enduring, including the scarcity of food: for this they loved him and were ready to follow him and his dreams of power and glory to the gates of Hades. Focusing on the food mentioned in the above excerpt from Caesar's own book, the *chara* he refers to must have been what known as *kelkasa* in the Albanian language, a wild tuber not too different from a potato, although others have seen in it an allusion to what Pliny calls *Lapsana*, some sort of wild cabbage.[55] This strongly testifies to the scarcity of food they were experiencing at the time. Another interesting element in that passage is the fact that, if presented with it, the soldiers would occasionally eat mutton. Could this mean that they, and eventually Caesar himself, got the parasite from that meat? If he ate the mutton, Julius Caesar likely did not swallow *Taenia solium* eggs, since their host is the pig. Another type of *Taenia*, *Taenia ovis*, is known to affect sheep, though it is not transmitted to humans.[56] Could other species of worms have been caught through consumption of undercooked lamb or mutton? Would they have caused epileptic seizures similar to those caused by *Taenia solium*? As said, *Echinococcus Granulosus* is a possibility, as its larval form is known to be present in ovines, too, but we have already pointed out that symptoms should have manifested earlier than the sources as read by McLachlan would suggest. Another chance is that, through ovine meat, *Fasciola hepatica*, another kind of worm, made its way into Julius Caesar's intestine but in that case the chances that it caused him to develop focal epilepsy are virtually non-existent since: i. it is a ubiquitous parasite but also very rare; ii. it can cause damage to the liver but never to the degree of portal hypertension, which as a consequence could lead to a severe brain condition known as hepatic encephalopathy; iii. although seizures are considered amongst differential diagnoses of hepatic encephalopathy, a clear clinical distinction can be made and, given that hepatic encephalopathy can easily progress to very grave stages up to coma, Caesar's generally good health clearly rules out any such eventuality.

Perhaps we will never be able to prove or disprove the fact that Caesar ingested swine meat containing *Taenia solium* eggs which eventually caused his alleged epilepsy, but, despite its medical relevance, we are of the opinion that neither chronology nor evidence from primary sources support this pathographic reconstruction of the facts.

Brain Tumour

This clinical possibility was first proposed in 1995 by Gomez and colleagues.[57] In their work they state their view that the epileptic fits were late onset ones and focus on the fact that the ancient sources report or imply personality changes and depression and certainly mention headaches. Having excluded an organic brain syndrome on the basis that Caesar attended a party in Cicero's home in December 45 BC and 'they departed at length without any mention of mental changes', the authors concluded that all those manifestations made it possible 'to propose an anatomic diagnosis of an intracranial lesion'.

By intracranial lesion, thus a focal lesion (ie localised in a particular area) they meant a brain tumour which they write 'may have been located above the tentorium in one of the cerebral hemispheres'. In more detail, they consider the mentioned headaches fundamental to their diagnosis in that they are persistent, so suggestive of an expansive lesion within the brain, and they note the fact that 'the duration of over two years suggests a benign lesion, slow growing in nature'. This timeframe, they conclude, strikingly differentiates benign lesions from brain abscesses and metastases from tumour primarily located in other body districts, for which a short term evolution (weeks, months maximum) would be the rule. For these reasons, symptoms and evolution in time they conclude that a convexity meningioma seems to be the better explanation for his late onset epilepsy. Taking a closer look at their hypotheses we should in the first place specify that meningioma are tumours arising from the meninges, the fibrous layers enwrapping the brain, in particular from arachnoid cells, those of which the *arachnoid meninge* (located between the outer layer called *dura mater* and the very thin inner layer called *pia mater*) consist. There are several type of meningioma: the type mentioned by the authors (convexity meningioma) grow from the surface of the brain, which, because of its shape, is a convexity and account for roughly twenty per cent of all cases of meningioma. As the authors write, the growth is very slow and eventually leads to masses of considerable size capable of displacing the brain and invading the bony surface of the skull; the basic symptoms this tumour would cause are convulsions and headaches. Within this same etiological field, Gomez and colleagues also gave a few differential diagnoses, such as astrocytoma and oligodendroglioma, the former originating from starry-shaped glial (non-neuronal support) cells within the brain (astrocytes), the latter being named after olygodendrocytes, another sort of glial component. Such causes would give a clinical spectrum almost identical as in the case of convexity meningioma.

This theory is medically quite interesting from both a neurological and historical perspective and it is somewhat hard to understand why it has been so seldom debated when compared to other far less credible and far-fetched possibilities. It suffers from two major limitations, though.

a. It greatly depends on that 'headache' mentioned by Plutarch in his general portrait of Caesar's health and character, while we know of no such reference by Suetonius or other sources. In spite of this, in a 1999 article Dr Jeffrey M Jones, somehow endorsing the 1995 diagnosis of brain tumour, historico-medically argues that 'This raises an interesting question as to whether history would have been different had Caesar not had such difficulties. History probably would not have changed, but Caesar's case does raise the issue of the occurrence of headaches with central nervous system tumours. This is the only example of famous people where headaches were probably secondary as opposed to primary.'[58] Basing most of the diagnosis on this reference to a headache can easily be shown to weaken the whole effort. In addition Plutarch's use of the words τὴν κεφαλὴν νοσώδης [tèn kephalèn nosódes] clearly points to a headache – the question is, which type of headache? As we said in the previous chapter, the collocation can be literally translated as 'ailing, sickly condition in the head' and only the tone used by the Greek author and the context of a general all-encompassing description in which it is put allow us to think of it as a condition that gripped him constantly and recurrently for at least some years (in the last part of his life). Scholars of ancient Roman medicine have delved into the matter and analysing Pliny's references have come to the conclusion that several definitions of headache were used: *cephalea, capitis dolores, capitis dolores fervoresque capitis dolores fervoresque, temporum Dolores,* and *cervicis Dolores* respectively referring to headaches in general, to ailments of the head, headache with heat, pain located to the temples or the nape.[59] The Greeks, furthermore, distinguished between *cephalgia*, a type of headache not lasting for a long time and *cephalea*, lasting much longer and being characterised by recurrence and becoming progressively more and more severe to the point of becoming particularly difficult to cope with on a daily basis. We can now fully see how vague the Plutarchean word choice is: the general context and tone would point to a cephalea, but then would Caesar have been able to resist so greatly hammering a pain? Would it not then be more sensible to look at headaches firstly as a possibility and secondly as an ancillary symptom, rather than one of the main ones? Moreover, in which cranial areas was the pain reported? Once more Plutarch's words help very little.

b. This hypothesis also consists of a bold venturing into the field of hyper-specific etiologies: if one can hardly be sure Caesar had epilepsy, then how can a sole symptom (headache) result in a diagnosis of a progressively growing benign tumour, and even more precisely a convexity meningioma or other similar neoplastic manifestations? More caution should indeed be implemented.

c. As underlined by McLachlan, it would be very unusual for such a lesion in the brain 'to present with infrequent seizures and remain otherwise asymptomatic for two years'.

Despite these difficulties, this hypothesis was produced again in 2010 by Dr Francois P Retief and Dr Johan F G Cilliers in an article published in *The South African Medical Journal*.[60] Since the authors do not reference the 1995 work in their bibliography they must have reached similar conclusions independently of the previous work. Discarding other causes as unlikely, they propose meningioma since it 'may indeed present with generalised epilepsy without other symptoms of cerebral disease, and progress very gradually in the course of many years. Generalised epilepsy is the first symptom in two-thirds of cases of meningioma.' They also explain that symptoms such as vomiting, headaches, visual deficit, dizziness, personality changes and mental deterioration could occur in such a clinical setting. 'With a lesion of the temporal lobe, amygdala or hippocampus' – 'a typical psychomotor or temporal lobe syndrome may arise: episodes of complex sensory and motor dysfunction characterised by speech defects, disordered thinking, automated aimless simple movements [...] and only generalised convulsions.' Some of these symptoms have undoubtedly been attested for Caesar and we certainly agree with the authors that Caesar's behaviour 'became erratic' at the end of his life. In addition, they also re-examine the episode that occurred during the battle of Thapsus (46 BC) in the light of temporal lobe epilepsy – namely the benign tumour they propose – since 'he apparently experienced warning symptoms of 'his illness' which lasted long enough for him to arrange for transfer to a safe place'. At the end of their dissertation, they also intriguingly suggest that 'terminal erratic behaviour might even have caused him to be unduly negligent about his own safety and so have aided his assassins on the Ides of March.' Unlike the 1995 proposal this hypothesis has the merit of being more cautious in its pursuit of an exact type of benign brain tumour and meningioma are mentioned in general terms. Nonetheless it is weakened by:

a. the fact that no clear choice of whether it was generalized or focal epilepsy is stated and both options are considered possibilities;
b. does not regard headaches as fundamental to the diagnosis, which helps to get rid of the philological and historical problems highlighted above but at the same time loses that strong correlation with growth over time

of the tumour evidenced by the progressive nature of the headache (as interpreted by Gomez and colleagues). The other symptoms, in particular the psychomotor one can have several etiologies, not necessarily brain tumour. In other words, the 1995 diagnosis was much more audacious and strongly depended on the unclear reference to headaches, but because of this was more historico-clinically weighty. The 2010 one is epistemologically better devised and more cautious and balanced in its approach but a little vaguer and less direct.

Hartnup Disease

Hartnup disease is a metabolic disorder of genetic nature, transmitted in an autosomal recessive fashion (ie one mutant allele in one of non-sex chromosomes is not sufficient to cause the manifestation of the disease, the so-called clinical phenotype). It primarily affects the absorption or nonpolar amino acids such as tryptophan, which once converted into niacin becomes essential to the formation of nicotinamide. Nicotinamide, a water-soluble vitamin belonging to B group, is vital to the formation of NAD+, which is a coenzyme fundamental in a number of key biochemical metabolic pathways within the cell. This pathological condition usually arises in childhood and consists of such symptoms as photosensitivity (extreme sensitivity to sunlight), nystagmus (an involuntary eye movement), intermittent ataxia (uncoordinated gait and movements) and tremor (trembling, shaking). A rash is a very common find in parts of the body exposed to sunlight, which together with other powerful stimuli, namely psycho-physical stress, fever and poor diet, can trigger symptomatic manifestations of this disease. Other signs such as headaches, fainting, mental retardation and psychiatric issues like delusions, hallucinations, mood alterations and anxiety may also be present. Nowadays this condition is treated by means of an integrative protein-rich diet and with neuropsychiatric treatment for those patients in whom the condition has severely worsened. On account of its familial and genetic nature, as well as of the important neuropsychiatric symptoms encountered, in 1986 Dr J H Dirckx proposed this as the explanation of most of the problems of the Julio-Claudian dynasty.[61] It makes sense to include this hypothesis in this section addressing secondary epilepsy, since, no matter the genetic nature of Hartnup disease, neurological problems (possibly including epilepsy) would be a secondary manifestation of a more general pathological condition.

The scholar considers an eminently masculine and imperial family tree, Caesar's ancestors and children being excluded along with female family members, but unlike the already discussed genetic hypothesis by Hughes, Dirckx also considers Augustus (63 BC–14 AD), Caesar's nephew and first Roman emperor. Now follows what Dirckx found in Julius Caesar, Augustus, Caligula (12–41 AD), Claudius (10 BC–54 AD) and Nero (37–68 AD).

Julius Caesar suffered from epilepsy and nightmares in adulthood and Dirckx specifically thinks that 'his first seizure at Corduba' occurred 'probably in his early thirties while he was serving as quaestor in Spain'.

Augustus had skin problems as highlighted by Suetonius where he says that he was *maculosus*, that is his skin had broken out in spots and 'over his chest and abdomen he had a cluster of birthmarks matching, in number and arrangement, the constellation of the Big Dipper' as well as 'patches of roughed skin which had been converted by scratching and by frequent vigorous use of the scraper [in the bath] into an impetigo.' Dirckx also pays attention to more passages in Suetonius' account in which it is written that the Emperor limped because of a weakness in his left hip but attributes this infirmity to an old injury. He then examines Suetonius' further allusion to more pathologies such as pain in the bladder, a disorder of the liver and numbness and stiffness in his right index finger, seasonal illnesses, oppression in the chest, catarrh and his intolerance of the sun 'even in winter'. The physician does not consider all of these problems the result of one disease and simply concludes that Augustus 'had dermatitis and took pains to protect himself from the sun', which fits the diagnosis of Hartnup disease.

Caligula is again analysed in the light of the portrait given by Suetonius: a monstrous being who loved torture, executions and incest, who in his boyhood suffered from *morbus comitialis* and who in adulthood continued to suffer from sudden fits. He is also described as mentally sick and suffering from severe insomnia, enjoying no more than three hours of sleep per night, tormented by odd nightmares. Moreover, Dirckx specifies that 'his behaviour was often bizarre and his emotions ungovernable.'

Claudius, whom – Dirckx epitomising Suetonius – 'Caligula had tolerated as a convenient butt for his practical jokes, a harmless nobody not worth murdering'. He succeeded the so called 'monster' but his health, mental status and ability to rule and administer an empire was treated with great scepticism by his contemporaries. Listing the symptoms reported by Suetonius (weak legs, grotesque manner of laughing, foaming at the mouth and nose dribbling when angry, stammer, terrible pains in the stomach), the author concludes that 'Claudius had a disturbance of gait, a stammer, involuntary movements of the head, and a tendency to drool under the influence of strong emotion'.

Nero is, in Dirckx's words 'the quintessential mad emperor' who 'outdid his uncle Caligula', a figure 'disgustingly vain', showing broken out and malodorous skin. He concludes that the emperor, the last representative of Julio-Claudian family, 'suffered delusions of grandeur and his behaviour was that of a psychotic'.

Finally, without drawing clear-cut conclusions, Dirckx reflects on the fact that marriage between close relatives and even a case of frank incest (Caligula having intercourse with his sisters, among whom Agrippina, Nero's mother) was a fact within the Julian house and highlights that this could have favoured 'the expression of recessive genetic traits'. Then, in a final attempt to incorporate the rest of the family, including women and unknown male members, into his scheme, he hurriedly argues: '[…] it must be observed that since Suetonius and other ancient writers devoted little attention to the histories of women of the Julian house other than Agrippina, Messalina and Augustus' daughter Julia […] one or more affected females in the family cannot be ruled out. Indeed, Agrippina herself was evidently mentally disturbed. Additionally, males of the Julian house besides the five who achieved imperial rank may perhaps have been affected; some of them are mere names to us, while others have no doubt altogether escaped the notice of history.' This type of final precaution is always welcome in historical debates but does not actually help very much to verify the possibility of

Hartnup disease, on the contrary it increases the number of untested clinical possibilities. This theory is very exciting and certainly catches the imagination of anyone fascinated by the laws of inheritance but at the same time is very unlikely since it suffers from serious historical, epistemological and medical limitations:

a. Attention is almost solely paid to male members of the Julio-Claudian family and Caesar's ancestors and children are excluded. In his article Dirckx states 'a glance at the genealogic chart shows that all the probands are male and all the (presumably unaffected) intermediaries are female'. This suggests, in his opinion, an X-linked recessive-type inheritance, but he also considers an autosomal recessive mode possible. The statement that all the intermediaries are unaffected females is too speculative and the family tree shown in his paper, which goes down from Caesar's father to Nero, only mentions three women (Caesar's mother Aurelia, Caesar's sister Julia Caesaris and Caesar's niece Atia). That no other women of the family are organically and fully discussed is hyper-selective and too much of a generalization to speak in definitive terms. In addition, the autosomal recessive mode of inheritance seems to be the more likely fashion in which this condition is passed down through the generations.

b. Augustus' health is examined in detail but Tiberius' (42 BC–37 AD), his successor and second Roman emperor, is not even mentioned. There is no sign of skin problems or other major signs of Hartnup disease in Julius Caesar's case or in his ancestors, yet the entire pathology is suggested to derive from him. Since the rash is vital to this hypothesis it makes sense to keep the whole Julio-Claudian family together, unlike when speaking of primary epilepsy with Julius Caesar either excluded or included, as the alleged epileptic trait in later emperors could easily be derived from the Claudian branch of the family, rather than from the Julian one. In Dirckx's view, the Claudian branch had basically no impact at all and the whole of the disease comes from Augustus, through Julius Caesar. Augustus was Caesar's nephew and political heir and the blood link was guaranteed through Atia, Caesar's niece and daughter of his sister Julia Caesaris (101 – 51 BC) and Marcus Atius Balbus (105 – 51 BC), but he was also the son of Gaius Octavius (100 – 59 BC). Can we be absolutely sure that if he really had Hartnup disease he did not inherit it from either his grandfather Marcus Atius Balbus or his father Gaius Octavius?

c. From a genetic point of view, selective attention is paid to the skin rash, only present in Augustus and Nero and frankly of an apparently different nature since, while Nero's skin is defined broken out in patches, Dirckx himself has to admit that 'the characterization of Nero's skin as maculosus is altogether too general to permit any conclusions to be drawn as to whether he too had a pellagra-like rash'. Clinically speaking, the choice to focus on Augustus' rash as a direct consequence of his being intolerant of the sun is very sound and interesting, nonetheless why avoid drawing any conclusion about his other many problems, such as index finger numbness, bladder and liver disorders? Could that rash be part of a more complex clinical picture? In addition, if that is the case, could the rash not be merely some skin condition proper to Augustus and not a key element to the reconstruction of a family tree of Hartnup disease?

d. As we saw, Hartnup disease is exacerbated by a number of stimuli and there is no doubt psychological stress affected men in charge of a colossal empire who were always defending their power from snares and conspiracies to overthrown them. Nevertheless, diet also plays a key role, since a protein rich one would compensate malabsorption of key amino acids, whose deficit is at the heart of Hartnup disease. The sources, even Suetonius, simply do not support the fact that Caesar, Augustus, Caligula, Claudius and Nero had such a diet as to trigger potent manifestation of Hartnup disease.

e. Dirckx is of the opinion that Julius Caesar suffered from epilepsy for the first time when he was in Spain as quaestor (69 BC), thus in his early thirties. As we argued in Chapter One, this is certainly a possibility but it would then conflict with Suetonius' statement that his disease started towards the end of his life, which is corroborated by more descriptions of faints and psychomotor changes. 31 years of age is a long way from 56, when he was killed. For this reason, the Corduba reference ought to be considered as 49 BC or 45 BC, the former being much more likely, since it allows a clear progressive sequence of pathological events, namely Corduba (49 BC), Thapsus (46 BC), 45-44 BC (incidents in Rome).

f. This hypothesis is based on one single historical source, Suetonius, and no comparison of analysed accounts is made with other Latin or Greek sources, thus the possibility of an accurate and cautious reassessment is greatly limited and etiologically framing, that is the confident formulation of a precise diagnosis is just a step too far from that which the available material veritably permit.

g. Hartnup disease is a very rare condition, affecting about 1 in 30,000 individuals, so before proposing it with confidence one should be totally sure about the family tree in which the disease purportedly developed. Even if such a tree is available (thus certain members of the family can be ruled out), simpler hypotheses involving much more common disease – possibly even documented and known at the time – ought to be considered in the first place, which does not seem to be the case here.

Temporal Lobe Epilepsy – Bursztajn's Interpretation

As an appendix to this chapter, we have chosen to include amongst our detailed discussion of potential causes of Caesar's alleged epilepsy the reflections presented by Professor Harold Bursztajn in 2003-2004. His work was done in cooperation with Italian Colonel Luciano Garofano, who at the time led the Parma forensic investigation centre (RIS, *Reparto Investigazioni Scientifiche*) and was shown in a 2003 documentary entitled *Who Killed Julius Caesar?*[62] Although this work has made its way into respected medical discussion, it looks as if the media and a little showy light around it, as well as the sometimes much too hurried conclusions it draws, have somehow prevented it from being included in traditional philological and historical debates. In our opinion, this work, with all its limitations, proved a milestone in assessing Caesar's behaviour during his last months and days in office and for the first time focused people's attention on the role of Caesar's own party and Caesar himself in his violent demise. Together with the recent discovery in Largo Argentina – in Rome, located where Pompey's Curia used to be – of the exact spot where Caesar was stabbed to death, this study is practically the only one to have attempted to radically advance knowledge about Caesar's life and final acts. It is no easy task since so much has already been written on the topic that the risk of repetition still scares off most people considering writing something of substance about the Roman leader.

On account of its behavioural and historical implications we shall incorporate it fully into our discourse in the last chapter of this book, but it is worth mentioning it now since the renowned Harvard psychiatrist also focused on Caesar's epilepsy in detail. Respecting the principle enunciated above, that when lacking multiple sources and enough evidence one should be very cautious about venturing into the field of causative hypotheses, he simply opted for late-onset epilepsy, specifically temporal lobe epilepsy. This type of epilepsy is a chronic condition characterised by recurrent epileptic seizures originating in the temporal lobe of the brain. Paying a great deal of attention to the episode in which Caesar is accused of behaving arrogantly for not standing up as sign of respect towards the senators approaching, and to the reference made by Cassius Dio that he did so to conceal an embarrassing attack of diarrhoea, the psychiatrist thinks that failure to rise, loosening of the bowels, passing out and the episode when 'he in an exaggerated fashion offered his throat to the Senators to be cut' would perfectly explain the psychophysical changes and consequences of seizures generated in the temporal lobe. In addition, he notes that 'if someone was grandiose to begin with they will become more grandiose' and observes that 'Caesar wrote incessantly, he was active incessantly, was seeking sexuality almost desperately' and concludes that all of this would be the portrait of 'somebody who was struggling with the effects of temporal lobe epilepsy'.[63]

This hypothesis has several merits and shows some solidity, psychiatric, behavioural, political and historical, yet, strictly clinically speaking, it suffers from at least three major limitations. Firstly, attributing Caesar's sexual appetite or unrestrained activity to his late-onset disease is just not supported by the sources which clearly state that he had been very active throughout his life and that his sexual exploits had been known for a long time before his late adult age. Secondly, hypothesizing that temporal lobe epilepsy enhanced them is logical but it appears to be an exaggeration. In addition, the episode in which it is said that he had diarrhoea, should be treated with much more caution since only Dio mentions this intestinal complication, thus it should not be made a pillar of one's theory. Thirdly, the idea that he became much more grandiose than he was to begin with is intriguing, but the primary sources do not support this extensively as no mention of extreme late grandiosity is ever made. One may perhaps look at his decision, at the time already in the public domain, to conquer the Parthian Empire, avenging Crassus' (115–53 BC) defeat at Carrhae, then to come back to Rome through the lands of the Scythians taking the Germanic tribes by surprise from the rear, as a clear example of grandiose planning, something similar to Napoleon's or Hitler's absurd dreams of world domination, or of a quick submission of Russia. Would that be too impossible and unachievable a plan for Caesar? Cicero was of this opinion on 24 May 44 BC, just over two months after Caesar's assassination, which he shared with his friend and correspondent Titus Pomponius Atticus (110–32 BC): 'If the situation remains as it appears to be now, I don't rejoice at the thought of the Ides of March. In fact, he would have never come back ...' This allusion is extremely interesting since it may be both a clear sceptical allusion to the patent unfeasibility of the military plan – the memory of Crassus' devastating defeat and his horrible death with molten gold being poured into his throat while still alive – or even a direct allusion to his health condition.[64]

As far as we are concerned, we believe that Caesar's grandiose behaviour might have been enhanced by his disease but not to the extent of radically upsizing it. Likewise, if it really was his goal to transform his dictatorship for life into an orientalized monarchy, we must retain the opinion that it was not disease that made him conceive such a grand plan. As we have had the opportunity to explain in the first chapter, Caesar's essential psychological traits, that is hyperactivity, thirst for glory and power, will to dominate and marked sexual appetite, can surely be attributed to the three major psychological imprintings he received and was exposed to in his infancy and adolescence: the low status his once glorious family was suffering, his father's sudden death and his becoming the head of the family, the gossip about his having conceded himself passively to king Nicomedes of Bythinia. These are the core elements at the heart of Caesar's personality, already present in him by the time he turned twenty and substantially unmodified until the last days of his life. The ancient sources on the contrary seem to stress the fact that his mood and behaviour was changing and that he was developing a certain degree of depression, whose impact on his life and political career we shall shortly examine in detail.

These are the explanations that have been put forward by scholars persuaded by the fact that sources strongly suggest that Caesar was epileptic. Temporarily accepting this assumption, we have scanned them all and highlighted what works and what does not work with them. Although we do not believe that Caesar was epileptic at all, if asked to blindly believe that Suetonian *'morbus comitialis'* and that Plutarchean *'epileptikoîs'*, we are certainly very critical of any hypothesis suggesting that he had primary epilepsy and that a family tree of epileptics can be traced. Other propositions prick our medical curiosity more but they fail to answer previously highlighted limitations, to rely on single sources, to exceed in precision in suggesting the exact cause given the scant material. The vascular hypothesis is very close to our view on the whole matter and we will discuss this in the fourth chapter but before moving to our own work, one extra step is still necessary to fully understand and try to solve this complex historical-biological problem. We have seen that the sources decreed the establishment of the epileptic theory and that their two thousand-year-old legacy had led learned scholars to put forward a great number of explanations for the real cause of this epilepsy. A question arises at this point. Has anyone ever questioned the 'epileptic dogma'? The next chapter will answer this question.

Chapter Three

Doubting Epilepsy in Recent Times: An Imperial and Clinical Approach

As a prelude to the next chapter where we will sum up all that has been discussed so far, radically overturning the philological foundations that have allowed the establishment of the epileptic theory, and finally present our own historico-clinical interpretation of the facts, we wish to offer a thorough overview of the research that since the nineteenth century has not contented itself with looking for the exact or most likely cause of an *a priori* accepted diagnosis of epilepsy, yet which has courageously questioned the very assumption that Julius Caesar really was an epileptic. The attempts to achieve that ambitious goal have been very few – four to be precise over the course of about 100 years; over 150 years, if we include our own 2015 study (and this very tome) – and the amount of material available for reassessment and discussion is really scant, thin articles and dissertations, not even comparable with the bevy of richly argued and spectacularly presented ones we explored in Chapter Two. For this reason, classical scholarship has spoken of negative views or scepticism about Caesar's epilepsy, yet no real 'school of thought' has ever had the opportunity to structure itself organically in the historical field, only finding some fertile humus in clinical discourse. Despite such an unfortunate verification, they do represent invaluable material in any serious debate on the health of Julius Caesar. It will, however, shortly appear evident how the presented counter-theories may not always satisfy historical and clinical criteria and, as we carefully did with the epileptic-accepting hypotheses discussed earlier, we will not fail to highlight them. Nonetheless, it is not the solution to Caesar's health that they propose which counts most here, it is what arguments they produced to underline the unlikelihood of Caesar having epilepsy that we aim to rediscover. With respect to this, we certainly took another path from these studies, but in questioning the very foundations of the epileptic castle, we have followed in their footsteps.

Napoleon III of France – Natural Weight Loss and Nervous Crises (1865–1866)

Although in the previous chapter we expressed our strong scepticism about Hughes's theory that a family tree of epilepsy may be identified in the Julio-Claudian house, we certainly acknowledge that the scholar's paper has two chief merits. One is the already cited attention for the first time properly paid to Caesar's ancestors; although Kanngiesser had already focused on the death of Caesar's father, Hughes also recalled the similar death of his great grandfather. We do not agree with the conclusion that Sudden Unexpected Death in Epilepsy (SUDEP) is the most likely diagnosis, yet bringing those two sudden deaths under the clinical and historical spotlight was undoubtedly a fundamental step. The other commendable aspect of that 2004 study is the richness of the bibliography, probably the most complete to have appeared both in historical and medical articles on the topic, before Montemurro et al.'s 2015 publication featuring a new diagnosis and a general review, and obviously this book which sums up the whole matter. Amongst a number of precious sources retrieved by Hughes is Napoleon III of France's, *Histoire de Jules César* (History of Julius Caesar) first published in 1865-1866.[1] We have already mentioned this book in Chapter One when describing Caesar's birth. Being a nineteenth-century volume, it may not meet the expected criteria of modern classical scholarship, yet it is still a goldmine of information and invaluable arguments on the life of the Roman general. It is also a rare exemplar, since it is the product of the mind of an imperial head of state who was not merely interested in Caesar's life for historiographic reasons, but also for political and psychological ones. The nephew and heir of Napoleon I (1769–1821), before becoming Emperor Napoleon III was the only elected president of the French Second Republic. Then in 1851 he implemented a military coup and declared himself ruler of France. His reign would be a very long one, until his defeat at Sedan (1870) at the hands of the rising Prussian power, which ended ultimately with the proclamation of a new Republic. Apart from the final military disaster that put an end to an otherwise successful imperial reign, a trait that he shares with his uncle, the rest of his career very closely resembles Caesar's and Napoleon I's.

The three leaders: i. claimed and boasted about noble descent but their actual status was far from prominent in society; ii. succeeded in rising from such conditions to the highest ranks of power; iii. were men of arms, who viewed military conquest as the road to power, success, fame and a position in posterity; iv. were ready to turn law and the state upside down in order to achieve their personal goals. Such being the background, we can certainly expect his work to have some degree of bias in that Caesar's life and deeds are to be read in the light of an inevitable comparison with his uncle's and his own.

The two-volume tome is so sedulous in reporting even the slightest minutiae of Caesar's life that considerations on his physical strength and reported health problems are very easy to find. Echoing the renowned descriptions found in Plutarch's and Suetonius' accounts, he depicts a marvellously insightful and informative portrait of Caesar, which we intend to analyse stepwise.

> 'To his natural qualities developed by a brilliant education, were added physical advantages. His tall stature, his rounded and well-proportioned limbs, stamped his person with a grace that distinguished him from all others. His mouth, small and regular, but with rather thick lips, gave a kindly expression to the lower part of his face, whilst his breadth of brow betoken the development of the intellectual faculties.'

This first excerpt interestingly agrees with a 1943 description of the Tusculum Bust by Maurizio Borda, which we recall for comparison:

> 'Everything, in this portrait, is clarity of style and coherence of shape, from the large skull to the high and genius-like forehead, to the triangular shape of the face.'[2]

And describing his smile:

> 'In this [ie Caesar's mouth] is found a great part of his expression: an ironic smile just enlightens, without showing it, the mystery of his sealed lips.'

Napoleon interestingly reaches the same conclusions about Caesar's peculiar smile, or more generally speaking, of the aspect and conformation of the lower part of his face. The two studies also agree in their description of a high brow, interpreted not only as a noble look, but also as a sign of his high intellectual faculties, the result of a hyper-developed frontal lobe. Here we see the influence of phrenology, the pseudoscience first developed by the German anatomist Franz Joseph Gall (1758–1828) which aimed to determine a person's psychological and intellectual attributes by means of a morphological external study of the skull. Later phrenology-influenced Lombrosian notions could also have had a part in the theoretical background and spirit in which that reference was written. In the light of contemporary medicine, we can only reaffirm that it is simply a morphological variable and it bears no pathological nor biologically 'superhuman' correlation. When describing Caesar's face, we do not know whether Napoleon III is simply imagining the Roman's facial traits from a mix of literary allusions and sculpted images he might recollect, or if he has one particular bust in mind. There is a possibility that, like Borda, he is also describing the Tusculum portrait, since it was excavated by his uncle Lucien Bonaparte (1775–1840)[3] in the Tusculum forum in 1825, but, it seemingly being the intra-vitam prototype for most (if not all) other later post-vitam busts, the French Emperor may well be thinking of other sculptures, from French or Roman collections.

Napoleon III's account then focuses on the changing appearance of Caesar's facial features, more strictly relevant to our investigation:

'His face was full, at least, in his youth; for his busts doubtless made towards the end of his life, his features are thinner, and bear traces of fatigue. He had a sonorous and penetrating voice, a noble gesture, and an air of dignity reigned all over his person.'

Thinner features are an intriguing observation in that it would appear that the French emperor acknowledges a certain alteration through time in the overall fatty padding and distribution in Caesar's face, which seems to be a direct conclusion drawn from Suetonius' allusion to the fact the his health deteriorated towards the end of his life (*tempore extremo*). The

Emperor patently links that to the shift from descriptions of Caesar having a 'somewhat full', 'rather plump' face (*ore plaulo pleniore*). As we remarked in Chapter One commenting on the Suetonian description, while there is no reason to doubt that ' rather plump' ought to refer to the face, rather than the mouth, it is of interest to understand what caused his face to appear plumper than normally expected? Was it its viscerocranial anatomy, which has always been an immutable characteristic until the introduction in recent times of maxillofacial surgical techniques, or was it a more malleable tissue, his flesh both in its muscular component and, in particular, in the fat accumulated primarily in his cheeks, chin and (neck) areas? The triangular-shaped face of the Tusculum portrait would exclude the former eventuality. We are then left with the possibility of a generalised loss of weight, with eminently localised effects on the face. Borda, too, seems to agree with it as he, with a poetic touch, philosophic-medically remarks:

'In the thinness of the face, limp tear ducts, deep wrinkles burrowing his face, tendinous neck, where the cartilaginous relief of the thyroid cartilage emerges, are the marks of an intensely lived life, in its alternation of enjoyments and sufferings: but more is reflected than the materialistic hedonism of the Epicurean, the ethical asceticism of the Stoic: not an abatement in senile decay, but the exhaustion in the heat of battle.'

The point now is, what caused this loss of weight? Napoleon III and Borda seem to agree on the physical strains on Caesar's body, after so many years of hard-fought campaigns and sacrifices around the known world. From this we gather that Napoleon III rules out the possibility that such deterioration was caused by disease. Life with its hardships was the sole culprit. Now, were one to deny stress, both physical and psychological, played any role in this thinning of Caesar's face, one would be far from the truth. The question at issue here is, was this the main factor, or was it something more properly pathological, some disease, even his alleged *morbus comitialis*, that resulted in such visible and tangible outcomes? We will try to answer this at the end of the chapter and when discussing our theory.

Further focusing on Caesar's physical strength and appearance, Napoleon III then reinterprets a Plutarchean passage a little freely:

'His constitution, at first delicate, became robust by a frugal regimen and the habit of exposing himself to the inclemency of the weather. Accustomed from his youth to all bodily exercises, he was a bold horseman, and bore privations and fatigues without difficulty.'

Which should be integrated with another few lines about his bodily constitution and willpower, which are both interesting and a clumsy attempt to conceal the Frenchman's admiration for the Roman general:

'We discover in Caesar, both physically and morally, two natures rarely united in the same person. He joined an aristocratic delicacy of body to the muscular constitution of the warrior; the love of luxury and the arts to a passion for military life, in all its simplicity and rudeness: in a word, he allied the elegance of manner which seduces with the energy of character which commands.'

We remember, however, that the Plutarchean passage goes like this:

'[...] he did not make his feeble health an excuse for soft living, but rather his military service a cure for his feeble health, since by wearisome journeys, simple diet, continuously sleeping in the open air, and enduring hardships, he fought off his trouble and kept his body strong against its attacks.'[4]

From this last passage it can certainly be inferred that Caesar grew stronger and more ready to sacrifice himself, but it is not easy to determine whether there was an increase in physical strength or body mass. It is just too vague a description and it can apply both to one's mettle and to one's muscular build. The French Emperor's use of word 'robust' is not clear either, since robustness can be either mental or physical, or a mixture of both. If we are to interpret the Plutarchean passage and Napoleon III's translation-interpretation in exclusively anatomical terms, then the idea that his body was well-built and his face rounder before he reached his fifties and started deteriorating would make much sense. It would also reinforce the observations made above on the loss of weight and thinning of the facial fatty tissue.

There are two problems to consider, though, which suggest caution:

i. we do not know exactly how much his body grew to 'robustness' from his youth to old age;

ii. even if he was well nourished and his muscles developed more mass and strength, facial fat could have been influenced by the rich and considerable diet typical of a man who indulged in the pleasures of life and attended many banquets, which is the exact opposite of the allusion to his 'simple diet'. 'Simple' certainly means that he was not particular about rich and refined dishes, making the best of the food the situations he found himself in offered. That this was the case is attested to by an anecdote told by Plutarch a few lines after the latest quoted passage. It features that Gaius Oppius,[5] whose works served as the basis for later accounts and the scene takes place in Milan: 'Of his indifference in regard to his diet the following circumstance also is brought in proof. When the host who was entertaining him in Mediolanum, Valerius Leo, served up asparagus dressed with myrrh instead of olive oil, Caesar ate of it without ado, and rebuked his friends when they showed displeasure. 'Surely,' said he, 'it were enough not to eat what you don't like; but he who finds fault with ill-breeding like this is ill-bred himself.'[6]

On account of this, the idea that the facial fat and thicker facial muscles could well have been a trait inherited from his ancestors and this was patent enough to give the impression of a rounder face, should be considered. He could have been generally thin, but still have had a tendency to more adipose distribution in the craniocervical district. This, of course, will remain speculative. In addition, it should be remarked that before the outbreak of the civil war, Caesar had been basically absent from Rome for eight years, thus the sacrifices sustained in Gaul might have caused a certain degree of wasting away.[7] This could have been caused by malnutrition and the stress of war. Returning to Italy and Rome after so long a time it is not unlikely that his thinner appearance caused people who had not seen him for a long time to come up with such impressions. If we consider also his rare presence in Rome over the course of the civil wars we have a period going from 58 to 45 BC (his presence being more stable in Rome after the final victory in Spain in 45 BC until his assassination on 15 March 44 BC), thirteen years. In so long a period of time many physical and psychological transformation are expected to happen, especially if, like Julius Caesar, one is not living a retired and quiet life in a cottage in the countryside. Caesar left for Gaul that he was 43 and came back much later, many things had happened in the meanwhile and a certain transformation was noted by his contemporaries. Now, to briefly expand on this, we have no indication that he suffered from any major disease during the Gallic wars and we will stick to the Plutarchean mention of the first attack in Corduba – most likely in our view of the facts 49 BC. However, it cannot be ruled out that in the last years of the war in Gaul (51, 50 BC) something may have happened to him, or that his body was undergoing the pathological transformations that would start manifesting themselves during the years of the civil wars. In that case the *morbus comitialis* he is reported to have had, would likely be the culprit and, as an alternative to stress and malnutrition, or even in combination with them, could also explain his thinner face. Napoleon III, nonetheless, does not seem to believe that Caesar suffered from a major disease. He writes:

'Habitually temperate, his health was impaired neither by excess of labour nor by excess of pleasure. However, on two occasions—the first at Corduba, the second at Thapsus—he was seized with nervous attacks, wrongly mistaken for epilepsy.'

Elaborating on this facial transformation, an interesting multidisciplinary 1986 article by Sergio Macchi and Giancarlo Reggi[8] focuses also on the dictator's neck by means of a detailed analysis of coins showing the effigy of Caesar, minted just a few months before his death or circulated shortly after his assassination. Those coins are very interesting, the authors maintain, because they portray Caesar's final appearance. They are of the opinion that the coins show a patent set of morphological traits, which are not found in other Roman coins:

'The neck shows a particular accentuation of skin folds, both transversally and, anteriorly, vertically, emphasising the laryngeal area. […] From an anatomical point of view the neck pleating is unequivocally of cutaneous origin: it covers the sternocleidomastoid muscle transversally, running in parallel lines. A vertical wrinkling, anteriorly, clearly highlights the laryngo-thyroideal protuberance. Finally, there is an accentuation of the orbicular musculature of the mouth, matched by the salience of the zygomatic arch.'

From this they draw conclusions not too dissimilar from the possibility of a major disease causing weight loss examined a moment ago while analysing what Napoleon III meant in his description of Caesar's face:

'The somatic characteristics described above, recurring in Caesarian effigies, are typically found when there is a remarkable organic deterioration, whatever its cause may be. As a matter of fact, skin wrinkles on the neck are originated by the disappearance of subcutaneous adipose tissue. Moreover, the loss of weight is confirmed by the accentuation of the vertical wrinkling laterally to the area of the larynx, and by the cavity which comes to be formed within the cheek, again because of the disappearance of subcutaneous fat, between the zygomatic bone and the peribuccal musculature. The slimmer dictator and the specific look that cachexia gave to the face must have been well known to those around Caesar […]'

This is a very acute observation and honestly much more relevant than Napoleon's, in that it broadens the focus onto the whole facial and cervical region. The authors' statement that changes in Caesar's face must have been noted by people from his circle confirms our already expressed assumption that, once back to Rome after so many years away, his face and overall appearance had deeply changed, conferring on him a slimmer look, which only his general energy and iron will power saved from being dubbed a 'weakness', at least until the very end of his life. Cachexia, also known as wasting syndrome, is a medical term describing a condition in which muscular atrophy, loss of weight, weakness and loss of appetite are common.

Its main cause is cancer, but is also seen as a comorbidity (ie in association with) other chronic diseases, namely chronic obstructive pulmonary disease, chronic kidney disease, cystic fibrosis, neurological diseases like Parkinson and Alzheimer, chronic obstructive pulmonary disease, stroke and so forth. The authors make superb use of the historical sources and their historical reconstruction is probably the best philological study ever published on the topic. Another merit is that they simply focus on semiological evidence from the coins without speculating on the cause of the cachexia: for this reason we believe their observations to be extremely relevant and that they deserve to be linked and compared to Napoleon III's observation. Throughout their study the authors pay paramount attention to the historical sources we also analysed at the beginning, primarily those accounts featuring him in Rome and showing either fainting, psychomotor changes, choleric outbursts. They accept the fact that Caesar was epileptic but also believe he must have had some other illness as well:

'In about 45 BC the dictator's health conditions worsened substantially. But what disease did he suffer from? Surely not from epilepsy alone, which does not cause bodily deterioration.'

In sum, loosely speaking their stance can be summarised as follows:

a.   Caesar was generally in good health for most of his life but during his last 12-15 months his symptoms severely worsened causing him to appear very different, especially in the face where he looked much thinner and worn-out.
b.   Coins minted in those months testify this and show prominent cachexia.
c.   He had probably had some other disease before, likely epilepsy, but this would not explain his physical decay.
d.   he must have had something else, otherwise the numismatically evident cachexia would have no explanation.

We feel most of the potential causes of cachexia can be excluded in Caesar's case since he was more or less well-functioning until the end. If cancer, for instance, is considered:

i. the possibility appears a step too far and the evidence from the sources does not suggest it;

ii. loss of appetite is not reported and in general Caesar did not eat much, so that may not be used to maintain this neoplastic stance;

iii. if trusted to have really occurred, the epilepsy then ought to be explained as a concomitant disease presenting:

Scenario 1. Before the final disease (i.e. cancer)

Or

Scenario 2. As a direct consequence of the final disease.

If scenario 1 is right, then the epilepsy would be either primary (genetic) or secondary (caused by another disease). Primary epilepsy is very unlikely. Of the etiologies presented in Chapter Two, only arteriovenous malformation (not arteriosclerosis because he preserved cognitive functions) and tumoral ones would fit this scenario.

If scenario 2 is correct, then the epilepsy would be caused by the disease developed from 45 BC and testified to by the coins, but this would be secondary neoplastic formations in the brain, in which case:

• the Corduba and Thapsus episodes simple would not have happened or would have been nothing like epilepsy;
• the tumoral metastasis colonising the brain and coming from another part of the body, would have been a malignant mass, rapidly destroying his health. However, even the authors who have put forward the diagnosis of a brain tumour (likely in the temporal lobe), clearly state that the substantially asymptomatic nature of that hypothesized tumour would point to its benign nature.

On account of this, if cachexia caused by cancer is considered, the only possible scenario that would meet all criteria is the following:

Step 1: Caesar has epileptic attacks before 45 BC and perhaps even later because of arteriosclerosis arteriovenous malformation or a benign brain tumour.

Step 2: Caesar develops cancer which causes him to lose considerable weight.

In any case, even this scenario has a couple of difficulties:

1. Cachexia is solely evident in coins, while the Tusculum bust and the literary sources even as interpreted by Napoleon III would point to a milder degree of weight loss. That his face and constitution had suffered from hardships was evident, but had such a high degree of deterioration been visible, much more would have been found in literary sources;
2. The psychomotor changes characteristic of the attacks that happened from 45 BC to his death appear so similar to the Thapsus and Corduba ones that a continuity between them seems logical.

In conclusion, too hurried conclusions ought not to be drawn from cachexia evidenced in coins. Moreover, a balance between ancient texts, evidence from the Tusculum bust and the coins should suggest the more accurate use of expressions like 'a certain degree of weight loss' in lieu of cachexia, associated with much more life-threatening conditions. The neurological condition which gripped Caesar in all likelihood caused his decline, behavioural and psychiatric, more than physical.

Let us now go back to Napoleon's III reflection of this famed neurological condition: *'Wrongly mistaken for epilepsy'*. These words, over 1900 years since the last events of Caesar's life took place appear to be the first ones questioning the epileptic assumption and tradition. What does the French Emperor mean by 'nervous attacks'? That expression used by Napoleon III looks so medically correct that we should expect a crystal-clear explanation. Nevertheless, it can mean almost everything and nothing at the same time and anyone, even without a medical qualification, could use it to define a wide spectrum of neurological symptoms. If one used that expression, one would not make any major diagnostic mistake, but one would still be far from an exact definition of the neurological condition. For this reason, this expression has been considered historically to be a popular diagnosis and was in this sense, purely rhetorical and not based in real scientific knowledge, that the Emperor adopted it. Given that a few lines above he used the (already deeply examined) word 'fatigue', we may be tempted to speculate that the two notions and their history are not too distantly related to one another. This would mean that 'nervous crises' could be translate as 'nervous or mental breakdown' a condition characterised by anxiety and depressive disorder and triggered by powerful stresses. The point is, though, that such a definition is the product of our modern understanding of neurobiology and psychology. Psychiatric classifications have been mutating so much and often over the past 150 years that definitions that in Napoleon III's time had a specific meaning, simply no longer serve that purpose and have either become obsolete terms, or have even be replaced by totally new ones. Making a quick historical digression, it is worthwhile to recall that nervous crises (French: *crises de nerfs, crises nerveuse*) were also described as neurasthenia, a term first introduced in this sense by the American physician George M Beard in 1869 in a study published in the Boston Medical and Surgical Journal under the title *Neurasthenia, or Neural Exhaustion.*[9] This neurological condition included fatigue, anxiety, headache, increased heart rate and blood pressure, depression and many more symptoms. Such abundance of clinical presentations just does not help us and we should also remark that Beard's publication emerged four years after the Emperor's work on Caesar, thus his imperial majesty is unlikely to have meant neurasthenia in exactly the same way as Beard, although its vagueness and ample choice of symptoms and clinical presentations might well allow us to hypothesize that by 'nervous crises' he meant something along those lines. Nowadays, loosely speaking just to give our readers an idea, we tend to look at non-epileptic nervous crises as sub-dividable into three groups, neurogenic, psychogenic and conversion ones. The first ones, a very common occurrence, are caused by several factors but in 90 per cent of cases their cause is a vaso-vagal (ie mediated by the vagus nerve) syncope, that is a transient loss of consciousness caused by very short generalised drop of oxygen concentration in the brain (anoxia) mediated by an excessive stimulation of the vagus nerve which induces inhibition on the heart, thus reducing heart rate and blood supply to the organs, including the brain.

The second ones, more often known as panic attacks, are triggered by a situation with strong unpleasant connotation: the patient is out of touch with reality and may appear unconscious, he may sweat, breath rapidly, have an increased heart rate and tremble. The third type of crises is the so-called conversion disorder (once referred to as hysteria), which is triggered by strong emotional stress and has grand mal epileptic seizures as its differential diagnosis. The patient falls to the ground but hardly ever injures himself and can show some convulsions, which at a closer exam are rather disorganised movements. Phenomena such as tongue biting or urinary incontinence (typical of epilepsy) are missing. Crises normally last longer than epileptic ones and at the end outburst of crying is common.

Why then nervous crises, episodes of psychophysical breakdown caused by unfathomable stressful situations instead of epilepsy? Napoleon III's statement is lapidary and is not accompanied by any ancillary gloss. The passage itself has notes but they are mere citations of the well-known ancient sources. It follows that only one solution is possible: Napoleon came to the conclusion that the available information on the alleged epileptic fits is scant, uncertain, contradictory and too vaguely described and so generic that even much more common and less pathologic – in his view – options could be considered. Nervous crises would, in his opinion, explain the reports on his health in a better way. Hughes, who has focused only on this last part of the above quoted Bonapartian passages, is by no means convinced by the Emperor's arguments and reckons that a political explanation would account for this substitution of epilepsy with nervous attacks. He unequivocally writes:

'It is understandable why Napoleon I and later his nephew, Napoleon III, would not subscribe to Caesar's epilepsy, especially because Emperor Napoleon I patterned much of his personal and military life after the great Caesar.'[10]

Hughes means that a diagnosis of epilepsy would have meant a stigma on his famous uncle Napoleon and, as a consequence, on the whole Bonaparte clan, including himself. Loosely speaking, epilepsy has since classical antiquity been considered a curse sent from divine entities, thus he who suffered from it could easily be ostracised by society and would be condemned to live an outcast's life. Later epileptic fits, because of their sudden and uncontrolled spasms and contractions of muscles, foaming at the mouth and many more such abrupt, violent and scary manifestations, would be associated with demonic possessions, hence further contributing to an already great mass of social black marks. Only decisive advances in neurological sciences and development of effective treatments eventually brought this condition to its natural realm, which is of organic brain dysfunction, leaving supernatural attributes out of the discussion. Epilepsy is nothing more than an alteration of electric rhythm in the brain. It originates in a focus, a specific brain area to subsequently spread to surrounding areas – potentially to both hemispheres as in the case of generalized or secondary generalized epilepsy – in a fashion not too dissimilar to the way earthquakes spread from their epicentre causing the release of mechanical energy into the surface of the planet. In spite of this, the stigma linked to epilepsy remained for a long time, until a few decades ago. On account of this Hughes's words would persuade anyone: how could an emperor like Napoleon III model his ambition and career on those of an epileptic? This would have meant diminishing the aura of nobility and grandeur the very name 'Caesar' conveys. Since the sources report in any case some neurological condition similar to epilepsy at least in its presentation, it must have been logical for him to turn epileptic seizures into epileptic-like nervous crises, a much more common and stress-related occurrence, which can develop in anyone, without him being necessarily affected by a major incapacitating or pitiful condition. In addition, since Napoleon I, as we said, had greatly made his life model Caesar and there were stories portraying him, too, as an epileptic, his nephew must have been strongly motivated to remove the epilepsy altogether from Caesar's life. This seems an easy and logical explanation given the stigma epilepsy carried, nevertheless just one year before Napoleon III's book, the Italian psychiatrist Cesare Lombroso (1835–1909) had published his work *Genio e Follia* (literally Genius and Madness)[11] in which neuropsychiatric conditions, including epilepsy, were linked to superhuman traits, like excellence in the arts and the struggle for power. The work had a tremendous impact on that generation and as with other pseudosciences such as Gall's phrenology or craniometrics-based scientific racism – even if largely discredited on account of its purely speculative bases – its effects may still be perceived in modern times. According to Lombroso epilepsy had gripped men like Caesar and Dante Alighieri (1265–1321) and many more, thus providing evidence for its association with genius. Sigmund Freud (1856–1939) would later express very negative views of Lombroso's theories, in that – the Austrian physician thought – he confused epilepsy with hysteria and believed it to be a component of artistic creation and political-military genius, instead of a simplification of physical performances.[12] In spite of that, Lombrosian ideas had a massive influence in the nineteenth century, so stating that Napoleon III undoubtedly got rid of the epileptic possibility in Caesar because his Caesar-resembling uncle had been rumoured to have suffered from it is too much of a simplification. Two options, in fact, are on the table:

a. to erase the epileptic possibility altogether because it was a pitiful condition and meant inability to rule;
b. to substitute it with a much more common disease like nervous crises, which had no such stigma attached to them, but which could likewise have been interpreted as signs of weakness or loss of control over the political situation. They may well represent stress, but what if they were signs of a general mental breakdown?

Option *b* thus allows us to wonder:

i. in political terms, would it be better to suffer from a shameful condition such as epilepsy was thought to be, but which happened independent of the person's behaviour, mental strength or willpower, had been associated with the divine sphere in the past, was also linked to great men of antiquity and genius by foremost scientists of the day.

Or instead

ii. a much more ordinary condition that anyone can experience, is not associated with either the divine or genius, testifies that a great leader easily breaks down when faced with great stress?

Would such a diagnosis reassure a country about the ability of their commander-in-chief to carry on his duties?

These points are no idle speculation and we will come back to them when discussing Caesar in Chapter Five.

Napoleon I's health conditions have been debated for a long time and every few years a new diagnosis is proposed, either about his alleged epilepsy, sexual health or ailments or – more frequently – about his death, namely was he poisoned or did a cancer take his life? Discussing the latter issue now would require at least two more volumes and a robust appendix, to say the least, but even for his epilepsy we doubt a thick chapter would be a satisfactory achievement. We will then limit ourselves to mentioning some of the most lucid observations on the matter. Hughes fully endorsed the diagnosis of epilepsy as he would later do with Caesar, in this case being inclined to secondary epilepsy, which is caused by a primary disease ultimately damaging the brain. He believes that gonorrhoea, a sexually transmitted disease, could have caused the seizures following urethral stricture:

> 'Such a urethral stricture is commonly a sequel to gonorrhoea. The usual symptoms of chronic uraemia include a sallow complexion and nearly everyone of Napoleon's biographers have emphasized this point, including the description of his "conjunctiva as yellow as a lemon".'[13]

He then makes epidemiological remarks to corroborate this interpretation:

> 'Epileptic seizures occur in about one-third of individuals with chronic renal failure and are usually generalized tonic–colonic attacks.'

And he concludes that Napoleon is likely to have had two neuropsychiatric problems at the same time:

> '[…] the evidence seems clear that Emperor Napoleon Bonaparte had psychogenic attacks, based on tremendous amounts of stress in his life, and also had epileptic attacks. For the latter he could blame Empress Josephine for giving him gonorrhoea, causing a severe urethral stricture resulting in a chronic uremic state and finally epileptic seizures.'

This proposition – much more agreeable and likely than the familial tree of epilepsy in the Julio-Claudian House – pushes us to some reflections.

a. If Napoleon I had both psychogenic crises caused by stress and gonorrhoea-induced epileptic seizures, did his nephew Napoleon III, who had him also in mind when writing about Caesar – consider both?
b. If so, would that mean that he did not substitute epilepsy with psychogenic crises ('nervous' in his own words) as we postulated above, rather that he simply got rid of one of them?
c. If so, was that simply a psychological and political choice, or a matter of fact statement, based on the fact that he knew that his uncle primarily, if not solely, had psychogenic crises and not epilepsy, which he ultimately believed had also been what happened to somebody very much like his uncle, namely Julius Caesar?

A straightforward answer is just not available, yet such theoretical enquiries show us how much more complicated than expected the Napoleonic reference and comparison are. To add a pinch of salt to an already complicated story within the main story, in 1958 Dr G Dragotti, as part of a comparative reassessment of the health conditions of Caesar and Napoleon, gave a different interpretation of the facts, underlining how the sources were not so trustworthy and a diagnosis of epilepsy could be utterly questioned:

'The rumour that Napoleon had had epileptic seizures had already spread by the time he had reached the apogee of his glory. In 1810 a book by the English Lewis Goldsmith appeared, in which it was told with great abundance of details that the emperor in 1807, while he was entertaining an intimate conversation with the actress George, was struck by an epileptic attack. The book met with great success and was translated in all the languages, but before the emperor's downfall nobody else admitted to have witnessed attacks of that disease. Afterwards there appeared publications by individuals who meant to denigrate or extoll that man destined to great deeds which either confirmed or denied such gossip. Constant, his famous butler, in the memoirs published in 1830, reports that a lady-in-waiting had said 'that Napoleon during the night of 9 September 1804 had been caught by a "nervous shock, or by an attack of the epilepsy he suffered from". Yet Constant seems not to be aware that Napoleon ever had any such attacks. Talleyrand, more explicit in his memoirs, recounts that one evening in September 1805, shortly after having dined with him he fell to the ground unconscious, agitating and foaming at the mouth. This is the only description of a real epileptic attack, but its reliability is more than doubtful given that it comes from a man who was very interested in denigrating the man he had betrayed when he was his minister. Opposite vague and suspicious evidence is the fact that none of his close friends have never claimed to have known that Napoleon suffered from seizures and certainly not suffered from them at St. Helena, where his health collapsed and there was no shortage of emotional enough causes to trigger the attacks. This is testified in their memoirs by his fellow prisoners, the jailer, and the doctors who succeeded in assisting him, who nonetheless spent a great time recording everything that appeared abnormal in the prisoner.'[14]

As this excerpt brilliantly demonstrates, the sources are not very clear or absolutely trustworthy, thus a diagnosis of epilepsy in Napoleon's case remains a strong possibility to be considered, but there can be no certainty.

Summary

Napoleon III's analysis of Caesar's health has merits:

i.   to have brought attention to the fact that Caesar's physical appearance changed over time and that signs of fatigue had deteriorated it; which is very important in analysing his fellow Romans' reaction to his changing look. However, the idea that he suffered from a major disease such as cancer that caused him to considerably lose weight in 45-44 BC, while very interesting and based on numismatic evidence, seems to go a little too far; from which we conclude that his final deterioration, probably caused by the disease in the sources referred to as *morbus comitialis*, had a greater impact on his behaviour and mood rather than on his body;

ii. to have questioned the very assumption that he was epileptic, offering an alternative explanation, and causing other researchers to expand on this.

And shortcomings:

iii. to say that the crises were purely psychogenic (nervous ones) seems overly simplistic;
iv. that it does suggest why the author thinks they were mistaken for nervous crises;
v. that Napoleon I's medical problems might have influenced his nephew's description of Caesar's problems, although the matter, as we have demonstrated, is much more complicated than thought.

Donnadieu – Simulation of Epilepsy (1934–1937)

Several decades after His Imperial Majesty's reflections, another Frenchman took a radical position on Caesar's epilepsy, denouncing the likelihood of the assumption and for the first time arguing the reasons in depth. His memoir, read in 1934 before the members of the *Société des Antiquaires de France* made a very important point from the opening lines:

> '*Il est admis sand discussion, sur le témoignage des auteurs anciens, que Jules César était épileptique.*'

> 'It is accepted without discussion, based upon the testimony of the ancient authors, that Julius Caesar was epileptic.'[15]

This is extremely relevant. While Napoleon III thought that nervous crises were mistaken for epileptic attacks in the past and were thus so reported by authors like Plutarch and Suetonius, Donnadieu goes one step further: those who have discussed Caesar's health have never questioned the very nature of those attacks, so all later comments on his disease were nothing more that research based on an *a priori* accepted fact, namely that he really was epileptic. After this initial remark, Donnadieu clearly recognises the implications of his work, which, given the historical relevance of the patient, will not be limited to the medical field:

> 'This research is not, as one might think, exclusively medical. For its conclusions, it produces one of the most interesting contributions to the psychology of Julius Caesar, of which it shows a particularly curious aspect by unveiling one of the means used by him or his partisans to achieve the realization of his political goals.'

In a radical and highly sceptical reading of the episodes mentioned by the historians, Donnadieu is clearly not persuaded by the evidence and cites Appian as an example of the fact that other than Plutarch's word we know nothing about the Corduba attack. He also expresses his scepticism about what is reported to have occurred when Caesar did not stand up to honour the senators:

> 'In fact there is no reason to believe the incident in the temple of Venus Genitrix, during which Caesar seated before the temple, refused to stand up when the senators as a whole came to present him some decrees which conferred the greatest honours on him. This incident is reported by Suetonius and by Dio Cassius, but it would not seem to have any relationship with the epilepsy Julius Caesar would suffer from. Suetonius speaks of an affront to the senate; Dio Cassius accuses both the blindness caused by the gods and 'a disease, sudden and which moreover denied Cesar's going back on foot from his forum to his *Domus Regia*.'

Afterwards, he ends up accepting the Suetonian and Plutarchean texts as the material to be used for his diagnosis and he articulates a polemical argument against the historian Paul Jacoby who believed in Caesar's epilepsy and had written in his *La Sélection chez l'homme*, (*Studies on selection in man*) that he believed Caesar to be an epileptic.

Let us rediscover this passage and take a microscopic look at it:

'We know the entire genealogy of C. Julius Caesar of the thirty-five members of his family known to us. It is not said by anybody that was suffering from some disease worthy of being noted; thus the Romans attached, as it is known, a great importance to health. Historians did not fail to mention the most insignificant diseases in prominent figures and it is utterly unlikely that they ignored or neglected to mention a hereditary condition, above all a neurosis, a psychopathy [ie a psychiatric condition] or epilepsy, in such a high-ranking family as that of the Julii – epilepsy, in particular, again because of the divine origin which was attributed to it and of the political importance that it had in Rome (*morbus comitialis*). And it may be supposed that Suetonius, that Saint Simon of Imperial Rome, this writer so meticulous that he has been denied the title of historian to grant him that of anecdotist, Suetonius, who gives details so precise that it had been possible to accuse him of immodesty, that this model biographer may have not mentioned a hereditary cerebral disease in the family of the first of his twelve Caesars? Moreover, we note that Plutarch does not show great guarantees of exactitude, above all in the minor details of Roman history and life; we also note that Suetonius does not say a single word, in his biography of C. Julius Caesar, about the disease which would have prevented the dictator from taking part in the battles of Thapsus and Corduba. When it is about Caesar's epilepsy, Suetonius is usually cited, who speaks of two attacks Caesar allegedly had; yet Suetonius underlines these two attacks not as examples of the manifestation of the disease, but as exceptional cases, and one of them is all but an attack of grande mal epilepsy [original French: *un accès de haut mal*]. In any case, on the contrary, it will result from Suetonius' account that those two attacks were unique in the dictator's life. We also note that he was bald and that he was in the habit of always going about with his head naked, as much in the frozen marshes of Belgium as under the burning sun of Spain and of Africa – a fact that alone could well explain the nature of the disease entirely otherwise than it has been done until the present time, and that in any case makes its hereditary character uniquely improbable. Suetonius says that C. Julius Caesar enjoyed a good health, a strong constitution and that he easily withstood toils and sacrifices of war and camp-life.'[16]

In his response to this, Donnadieu rather ironically underlines:

'Dr Paul Jacoby [...] wrote that Caesar was epileptic. Plutarch, Dio Cassius and Celsius, he says, state it. Nevertheless, since this is a matter of hereditary disease, it is surprising not to find cases of epilepsy in the dictator's ancestors and, he attributes to the burning sun of Spain and Africa the nervous attacks shown by Julius Caesar, who was in the habit of walking bare-headed. One cannot side with Dr Jacoby's opinion, the symptoms of epilepsy are different from those of sunstroke. No confusion is possible.'

First of all, both passages add some medical information to the debate since they allude to Caesar exposing his head to the hot sun. It is likely that the ancient sources the French authors used is again Suetonius:

'On the march he headed his army, sometimes on horseback, but oftener on foot, bareheaded both in the heat of the sun and in rain.' [Latin *capite detecto, seu sol seu imber esset*].[17]

Absorbing so much heat would certainly have had an impact on Caesar's health since body temperature is considered normal up to 37.7C, beyond which limit an impairment of heat homeostasis becomes evident. In Caesar's case, this would be the most common occurrence simply caused by an excessive absorption of heat from the environment, and no internal neurological deregulation of the centres responsible for body temperature could be taken into account. Donnadieu's remarks that confusion is not possible are certainly correct – the very situation, increase in body temperature caused by extreme heat would surely have been recorded in the sources. Also, it would not explain why, excluding the Corduba and African incidents, he had four episodes when back in Rome, in quite different weather and conditions from those Jacoby describes (ie the long marches under the sun). Symptoms of sunstroke would, however, resemble in some ways those of epilepsy or other diseases (muscle weakness, nausea and vomiting, rapid heartbeat, confusion, headache, dizziness and even seizures), yet no mention of fever, or lack of sweating despite very high temperatures is made. In addition, despite certain similarities, the two conditions can be easily distinguished clinically. While such exposure to heat could have caused him some problems, nobody would have spoken of a disease which gripped him for years, since they would have immediately understood the triviality and ordinariness of the pathological occurrence. In other words, had he really fallen or had certain symptoms because of sunstroke, the sources would either have ignored the incidents as irrelevant to the historical discussion or they would have never linked them to his alleged *morbus comitialis*.

Despite Donnadieu's impeccable reply to the very idea that Caesar had epileptic attacks or epileptic-like attacks caused by sunstroke, the quoted passage by Jacoby is not that bad and some good points are made, which we list here:

a. Plutarch is good for general information but nor for minor details about Roman life and customs: he's a Greek and describes an alien culture;
b. Suetonius excels in reporting gossip so if Caesar really had epileptic attacks he would have written much more, or at least added something more precise to his sources;
c. *Morbus comitialis* had some association with the divine sphere in ancient Rome;
d. Jacoby's main aim was to '[…] examine whether the disease and the depravity of Julius Caesar may not permit to posit the existence of the hereditary neuropathic element in the family of Octavian Augustus'. To prove that this is not the case he discusses Caesar's health and concludes that an inherited epilepsy in the Julian house is '*singulièrment improbable*', 'uniquely improbable'. This is of great relevance, since it testifies that long before recent attempts to describe inherited conditions in the Julio-Claudian house either as being primary epilepsy [Hughes, 2004] or causing it secondarily [Dirckx, 1986], nineteenth century scholars insisted that there must have been a neurological genetic element in the ruling Roman family and that it had to descend *directly* from Julius Caesar. We have already expressed at length our stance on such interpretations, but the words of Jacoby must also be taken into account with respect to that specific debate.

Apart from these merits – and completely wrong diagnosis justly underlined by Donnadieu – one major point seems to be incorrect or extreme in its conclusions. To state that Suetonius does not say that his alleged disease prevented Caesar from taking part in the battles of Thapsus and Corduba, and that those were therefore exceptional occurrences, is an exaggeration. Suetonius mentions a decay *tempore extremo* (towards the end of his life). It can be argued that details and descriptions are not rich and frequent enough to justify the epileptic assumption but certainly a degree of pathology, probably milder than a manifest epilepsy, was present.

Going back to Donnadieu's study, after much polemical argument against Jacoby, the author attacks the epileptic assumption using both a constitutional argument and a psychological-political one.

The constitutional argument draws on the idea – now largely discredited – that an epileptic's face was recognizable, implying that a neurological condition like epilepsy could be detected through facial traits. Some psychological aspects, on the contrary, have somehow survived in medical discourse, but have become very marginal. Donnadieu affirms that epilepsy is normally associated with asymmetries and conformational defects of the ears, the teeth, of the mandible, which witness a degeneration. However he specifies that one of those defects is not enough to make a diagnosis of epilepsy and only their association, together with neurological manifestations would make that possible. He then argues:

'Caesar's iconography, of which the coins minted in his image constitute the most solid basis, witnesses the absence of facial anomalies in the dictator. [...] The slightly idealised, but how expressive, head in the Naples Museum shows a very marked, determined, a little haughty and disillusioned personality, but totally lacking any degenerative anomaly.'

And, exploring the dictator's psychology, concludes that, unlike the typical epileptic patient's, which is characterized by imbalance of most mental faculties and behavioural and mood disorders, Caesar's was the exact opposite:

'As a matter of fact, Julius Caesar comes across, in all the acts of his life and ardent youth, as endowed with a great intelligence, with a discernment and perseverance that permitted him to achieve all his political goals he had very early set himself.'

On the one hand, such ideas are both difficult to defend in modern medicine and, as far as our study is concerned, certain of them seem a little extreme, for instance the fact that Caesar was perfectly fine and had no changes in his mood and behaviour. The psychological-political ones, on the other hand, while still very extreme in the conclusion, are much more sensible and worthy of mention. Since we will cover them again in the last chapter because of their relevance in the discussion on why the epileptic theory has been so successful for such a long time in spite of scant evidence, we shall only briefly touch upon it here.

In brief, Donnadieu, separates the Thapsus episode (and perhaps even the Corduba one) from the later incident in Rome. He calls them momentary weakness in an otherwise robust and healthy body. He then argues that Caesar simulated his crises, making people believe that he was suffering from epilepsy, because that was a 'supernatural disease, characterised by strange symptoms, the morbus comitialis, which marked him who suffered from it of a divine condition [French: *du sceau de la divinité*]; he would become the creature of the gods, their instrument; he would somehow participate in divine nature; the same essence of the disease, the divine spirit entered [French: *soufflait*] him, manifested itself through him.' He avoided doing it before his troops because it would have been too risky, but he implemented it in the Roman political arena.

The idea that Caesar had no disease at all and that he simulated the attacks seems just too extreme and not entirely supported by the evidence, yet the psychological reflections put forward by Donnadieu are of capital importance and will partly be incorporated in our own reasoning.

Summary
Donnadieu's theory has the merits:

a. of introducing the psychological and political element as one of the explanations for why Caesar was called an epileptic;
b. of elaborating on *morbus comitialis* (interpreted as actual epilepsy), highlighting its relationship with the divine sphere;
c. of keeping stressing the lack of strong evidence in the sources to maintain that he really suffered from epilepsy.

And the questionable shortcomings:

d. to have based medical arguments mainly on the psychophysical constitution of epileptics, as conceived in his time;
e. to separate the Corduba and Thapsus incidents from the rest of the pathology;
f. to think that it was a simulation, which is intriguing as a hypothesis, but just too extreme and once again contradicted by Suetonius and other accounts testifying his problems before his death.

Cawthorne – Ménière's Disease (1957)

Following Donnadieu's position, Dr Terence Cawthorne published an article entitled *Julius Caesar and the Falling Sickness* in the *History of Medicine* section of the *Proceedings of the Royal Society of Medicine*,[18] which is still regarded as the most direct attack on the epileptic theory – before or since. In his article Cawthorne confesses to have had the inspiration from a reading of Shakespeare's *Julius Caesar*:

> 'The idea for this paper came when I was re-reading Shakespeare's "Julius Caesar" at the time when I was preparing an article on Ménière's disease.'

We may well imagine what the final diagnosis would be. Ménière's disease (after its discoverer, the French physician Prosper Menière – 1799–1862) is a disease of the inner ear causing symptoms such as rotational (spinning) vertigo, a sense of pressure in one's ear, progressive hearing loss, tinnitus (a noise or ringing in the ears not associated with a real noise or sound coming from the environment). This chronic condition usually affects people from 20 to 50 years of age normally involving one ear. Other symptoms like nausea, vomiting and sweating are common, and the direct resemblance to Caesar's symptoms as we have seen them in the sources is provided by sudden falls without loss of consciousness (present in a small percentage of affected patients) and migraine. These two symptoms nonetheless are not those Cawthorne focused on when formulating his diagnosis.

In his words, he found a very interesting reference to deafness in the following scene from Shakespeare's tragedy, a reinterpretation of the Lupercalia incident when Mark Antony offers Caesar a crown, but the dictator refuses it:

'*Cæs. Antonius!*
  Ant. Cæsar?

  Cæs. Let me have men about me that are fat:
Sleek-headed men and such as sleep o' nights:
Yond Cassius has a lean and hungry look;
He thinks too much: such men are dangerous.

  Ant. Fear him not, Cæsar; he's not dangerous;
He is a noble Roman and well given.

  Cæs. Would he were fatter! But I fear him not:
Yet if my name were liable to fear,
I do not know the man I should avoid
So soon as that spare Cassius. He reads much;
He is a great observer and he looks
Quite through the deeds of men; he loves no plays,
As thou dost, Antony; he hears no music;
Seldom he smiles, and smiles in such a sort
As if he mock'd himself and scorn'd his spirit
That could be moved to smile at any thing.
Such men as he be never at heart's ease

Whiles they behold a greater than themselves,
And therefore are they very dangerous.
I rather tell thee what is to be fear'd
Than what I fear; for always I am Cæsar.
Come on my right hand, for this ear is deaf,
And tell me truly what thou think'st of him.

[Sennet. Exeunt Cæsar and all his
Train, but Casca.
Casca. You pull'd me by the cloak; would you speak with me?
Bru. Ay, Casca; tell us what hath chanced to-day,
That Cæsar looks so sad.
Casca. Why, you were with him, were you not?
Bru. I should not then ask Casca what had chanced.
Casca. Why, there was a crown offered him: and being offered him, he
put it by with the back of his hand, thus; and then the people fell a-shouting.
Bru. What was the second noise for?
Casca. Why, for that too.
Cas. They shouted thrice: what was the last cry for?
Casca. Why, for that too.
Bru. Was the crown offered him thrice?
Casca. Ay, marry, was't, and he put it by thrice, every time gentler than
other, and at every putting-by mine honest neighbours shouted.
Cas. Who offered him the crown?
Casca. Why, Antony.
Bru. Tell us the manner of it, gentle Casca.
Casca. I can as well be hanged as tell the manner of it: it was mere foolery;
I did not mark it. I saw Mark Antony offer him a crown;—yet 't was not
a crown neither, 't was one of these coronets;—and, as I told you, he put it
by once: but, for all that, to my thinking, he would fain have had it. Then
he offered it to him again; then he put it by again: but, to my thinking, he
was very loath to lay his fingers off it. And then he offered it the third time;
he put it the third time by: and still as he refused it, the rabblement hooted
and clapped their chapped hands and threw up their sweaty night-caps and
uttered such a deal of stinking breath **because Cæsar refused the crown**

that it had almost choked Cæsar; for he swounded and fell down at
it: and for mine own part, I durst not laugh, for fear of opening my lips and
receiving the bad air.

Cas. But, soft, I pray you: what, did Cæsar swound?

Casca. He fell down in the market-place, and foamed at mouth,
and was speechless.

Bru. 'T is very like: he hath the falling sickness.

Cas. No, Cæsar hath it not; but you and I and honest Casca, we have the
falling sickness.

Casca. I know not what you mean by that; but, I am sure, Cæsar fell
down. If the tag-rag people did not clap him and hiss him, according as he
pleased and displeased them, as they use to do the players in the theatre, I
am no true man.

Bru. What said he when he came unto himself?

Casca. Marry, before he fell down, when he perceived the common herd
was glad he refused the crown, he plucked me ope his doublet and offered
them his throat to cut. An I had been a man of any occupation, if I would
not have taken him at a word, I would I might go to hell among the rogues.
And so he fell. When he came to himself again, he said, If he had done
or said any thing amiss, he desired their worships to think it was his
infirmity. Three or four wenches, where I stood, cried 'Alas, good soul!'
and forgave him with all their hearts: but there's no heed to be taken of
them; if Cæsar had stabbed their mothers, they would have done no less.'[19]

As discussed in Chapter One, the Lupercalia incident and its aftermath
certainly show some degree of rage and loss of control by Caesar, but they
are not a clear description of psychomotor changes as, for instance, his
reaction to Cicero's oration or, albeit disputed by scholars, the one in the
Temple of Venus Genitrix/Rostra[20] where he did not stand up to honour
the senators. An episode as described by Shakespeare never occurred at the
Lupercalia: the English author probably mingled together the story of the
offer of the crown which really took place with something else, probably a
known description of a typical epileptic attack. Cawthorne, too, contributes
to the confusion by referring to Caesar's apologies about his disease (that
in his words causes trembling, dimness and giddiness) in the aftermath of

the offer of the crown (*Lupercalia*) (Plut. *Caes.* 61), while it directly follows (Plut. *Caes.* 60) the Temple/Rostra incident.

Those lines witness the genius of William Shakespeare and have become immortal. Apart from details about potential conspirators and those who might betray him, they contain three references to Caesar's health:

i. **Deafness**: *Come on my right hand, for this ear is deaf.* Shakespeare's Caesar is suggesting that his left ear is deaf. The playwright's words are not to be read as a medical document, but it is in any case interesting to note that he says 'is deaf', not 'is becoming deaf, or is almost deaf'. This would mean that, if the Ménière's disease suggested by Cawthorne, were to be believed, then – the deafness being total – one should suspect that Caesar has suffered from the condition already for several years, but it would conflict with the Suetonian 'towards the end of his life'. In any case this is a fictional reinterpretation, not a biography nor a historical account.

ii. **Main Disease**: 'fell down', 'foamed at mouth', 'was speechless'. A description of major epileptic symptoms is given. Shakespeare somehow ends up filling the gap in the sources' vague descriptions.

iii. **Morbus Comitalis?**: 'he hath the falling sickness'. Shakespeare accepts the association *morbus comitialis* – epilepsy as a general rule – and brings it to the extreme by describing one of its strongest and visually impressive manifestations. It might be that he was also heavily influenced by Plutarch's own words, 'epileptic fits'.

Shakespeare seems to equate *morbus comitialis* with a full-blown epileptic attack, as tradition probably suggested to him, and describes the attack in detail, highlighting the tremendous effects it would cause, falling, foam at the mouth and loss of the speech. Furthermore, without directly linking to such a powerful pathological presentation, he also mentions a unilateral deafness. This, Cawthorne underlines, would be a direct hint to Ménière's disease. Commenting in general on the reliability of Shakespeare's words, Hughes expressed his admiring scepticism:

'Although the world honours Shakespeare for his enlightening and engaging plays, he cannot be considered an authority on the seizures of Caesar and, as a playwright, likely did take "editorial license" with the real facts.'[21]

We certainly agree on such a statement and are of the opinion that it can be extended to the mentioned deafness, too. Yet the problem is: where did Shakespeare take the allusion to deafness from? His source was Plutarch, and as we have seen, he does mention epileptic fits, but no deafness or loss of hearing. Cawthorne acknowledges this limitation:

'Shakespeare's source of information about Julius Caesar came from Sir Thomas North's translation of *Plutarch's Lives*; and it was Sir Thomas North who coined the term 'the falling sickness'. He did not translate direct from the Greek, but from the French of James Amyot, Bishop of Auxerre. There is no mention in Plutarch, or in any other Greek or Roman author, of Caesar being deaf, even in one ear.'

Even after checking the French version of Plutarch's *Life of Caesar*,[22] we can find no reference whatsoever to support the idea that, over the transposition from the Greek original to Sir Thomas North's (1535–1601) through Bishop Amyot's (1513–1593) version, either the description of the *Lupercalia* episode had been enriched with details such as foaming at the mouth or, throughout the text, any reference to deafness had been added. Assessing the part of Cawthorne's theory specifically dealing with Caesar's Shakespearean deafness and his introduction into the story, it is worthwhile to read the author's personal opinion:

'Where, then, did Shakespeare get his reference to Julius Caesar being deaf in the left ear? [...] Again, could it be that Caesar was suggesting that he was going to forget what had just been said? But as he had just been doing all the talking and very little listening, there is little point in this suggestion. As there does not appear to be any mention of Caesar being deaf in any of the references available to Shakespeare he may have put this in so as to add a touch of realism to the part. We know that Shakespeare always made his great historical figures behave like ordinary human beings; and indeed it is just that homely touch which makes his characters live. It could well be that Shakespeare knew someone or possibly more than one person who was troubled with the 'falling sickness' and deafness, and that he introduced the deafness in one ear in order to make Caesar like other men. […]'

This stance is based on common sense and has a logic of its own, yet it shows some weakness. A more persuasive interpretation is what some scholars have found in a passage in Caesar's parallel life, that of Alexander the Great:

'It is said, too, that at first, when he was trying capital cases, he would put his hand over one of his ears while the accuser was speaking, that he might keep it free and unprejudiced for the accused.'[23]

We cannot exclude that Shakespeare read these words in the *Life of Alexander* and, in a pathological or behavioural sense, attributed them to Julius Caesar, too.[24] More information on how this association may have been born are given by Cawthorne himself:

'The only reference I can find to Julius Caesar's deafness comes from George Wherry in *Notes and Queries* (1909), Series 10, Vol. XL, p. 243. "Julius Cesar's Deafness – Shakespeare makes Julius Caesar deaf in the left ear. […] It is quite possible that attacks of giddiness associated with Meniere's disease of the ear may have been mistaken for epilepsy. The Romans were familiar enough with epilepsy, which they called *morbus comitialis*, from the attacks witnessed in the Forum or Senate House which broke up the Assembly; and it is unlikely that aural vertigo was understood at that time."'

This 1909 reference is actually of the utmost importance in that it questions the Romans' ability to distinguish different forms of diseases with a clinical presentation somehow resembling epilepsy, in particular those involving falls or losses of consciousness. In other words, the notion that *morbus comitialis* always meant *epilepsy* is put forward. While his diagnosis of Ménière's disease is patently very unlikely to be correct, Cawthorne's more general reflections, largely based on this note, are of capital importance.

i. **He reaffirms that there has been more speculation about Caesar's epilepsy than can be found in the ancient texts.** He gets his message across in the first place through a general portrait of the dictator: 'As a young man he was undersized and delicate, but he grew up to be virile, tough and even licentious. [...] Always in the public eye, any disorder, infirmity or even slight accident is sure to have been noted and even magnified. We have heard of his baldness and of his amours, and even when he stumbled and fell when disembarking on to African soil during the Civil War this was noted by Plutarch. I am sure that if he had been subject to real epileptic fits we would have heard much more about them than has come down to us from the writers of those times.'

And in the second place by means of a logical conclusion: 'Had Caesar suffered from major epileptic seizures, these sensational attacks would have not been passed over so lightly by the careful biographer Plutarch, or by the gossip Suetonius.'

ii. **He finds the reported symptoms not to be suggestive of epilepsy and much milder in presentation:** 'It may be noted that in none of these three statements [ie the Plutarchean references to a. his general health, b. Thapsus, c. Temple of Venus Genitrix/Rostra (loosely interpreted as the Lupercalia incident by Cawthorne)] is there any reference to loss of consciousness, to foaming at the mouth, to twitching of the face or limbs, or indeed to any of the other manifestations of epilepsy.'

Summary
Chief merits:

g. Cawthorne's work skilfully highlights the main issues with the diagnosis of epilepsy, stressing the fact that very limited information and scant and unspecific descriptions of his epileptic attacks posit a serious problem with the assumption that he certainly suffered from epilepsy;

h. if he really had epilepsy, then more accounts would have been written and typical manifestations of that disease would have undoubtedly been recorded, given the character's prominence;

i.   *morbus comitialis* had a broader meaning than epilepsy alone.

Major Limitations:

j.   he mainly uses Plutarch as his source and investigates the transmission of the text from the Greek to North's English translation, but other sources should have been discussed more thoroughly;

k.   his alternative diagnosis is largely based not even on a secondary source but on a sixteenth-century play in which Shakespeare's poetic licence heavily deforms the facts as told by the ancient historians.

Coming to the end of this chapter, we have fully examined the treated subject and are ready to draw conclusions and present our alternative theory: multiple mini strokes in a patient with likely family history of cardiovascular disease.

Chapter Four

A Simpler Hypothesis and a Novel Idea

At this point of our study we have been through so much information and so many theories that a little recap will not harm anyone. Let us summarise the information we have and focus on epilepsy and its likelihood and perception. This will lead us to our alternative diagnostic proposal. As a disclaimer, we would like our readers to know that this chapter will be thinner than the preceding ones and the following one, since our theory consists of much simpler reasoning which shows up after the *pars destruens* has been completed, that is once limitations of other theories and issues in the original sources are stressed. In our view most theories that have been proposed so far have exceeded the facts in their quest for absolute diagnostic precision, when the evidence provided by the ancient authors is instead extremely limited and the symptoms are vaguely described. As a first step one should try to understand if Caesar really had epilepsy and, if not, what other anatomical district or physiological system may have been affected. After that, and only after that, pondering on the likelihood of all etiologies and comparing their normally observed outcomes in modern patients with the same history, a cautious diagnosis may be formulated.

The sources suggest the following evidence:

Julius Caesar enjoyed good health for most of his life and no major disease or sign of epileptic disease can be found in accounts of his life prior to the start of the Civil War. Although not perfectly coinciding, almost all the sources, either directly or indirectly, point to the fact that he started having health issues with varied symptoms (faints, dizziness, psychomotor changes, headache, nightmares, choleric outbursts, etc.) towards the end of his life, which the authors call *morbus comitialis*/epilepsy. Descriptions, nevertheless, appear to be rather vague and clear-cut descriptions of typical epileptic attacks are missing. The only one could be Thapsus, even if the symptomatology is not so severe and other sources even say that he took part in the battle. In addition, family history of epilepsy is defective or highly speculative in his ancestors and offspring and only more consistent in late (post-Augustan) descendants, in whom not only the Julian blood flowed, but also the Claudian one. On the contrary, re-examining his ancestors' sudden deaths, the terminology adopted by Plinius, the almost identical presentation and the logical and clinical likelihood (they being reported not to have suffered from an infectious disease or to have been killed violently) it seems that, while no definitive conclusions may be drawn, a cardiovascular explanation is a more probable eventuality.

From which it follows that:

The general impression one gets from this clinical picture (anamnesis in medical jargon) is that Caesar did not suffer from primary (genetic) epilepsy and that, if he really had it, he must have developed it later in life as a consequence of another disease.

However, after examining all of the proposed possibilities, serious chronological, historical, philological, methodological and clinical issues have been highlighted in Chapter Two which put those hypotheses at risk. Of the proposals which show fewer or none of these problems, the two most likely (and less far-fetched) are those based in logical thought, frequency of diseases and clinical common sense, namely head trauma (military activity variant) and cardiovascular disease (arteriosclerosis and arteriovenous malformation). A major head trauma, however, is not recorded in the ancient sources, while for the other two hypotheses, there is the recorded evidence of the sudden apoplexy-suggesting in two of his ancestors.

Furthermore, although the sources call those episodes 'epilepsy' (the Greek-language authors) and *morbus comitialis* (Suetonius), can we be absolutely sure that the diagnostic precision in those days was so advanced as to allow a clear distinction between a classical epileptic presentation and epileptic-resembling conditions? Even nowadays that clinical knowledge has progressed to a degree of excellence never before seen in history, epilepsy may trick clinicians and a long list of differential diagnoses have to be considered and ruled out before formulating a firm diagnosis of epilepsy. Those differential diagnoses are principally: syncope, migraines, panic attacks, psychogenic seizures, vascular conditions, movement disorders, sleep disorders such as narcolepsy, Mènière's disease. Although the expression *morbus comitialis* (ie disease of the assembly hall) was associated with a divine curse and meant the suspension of an assembly because it was regarded as a bad omen, and most certainly represented epilepsy, can one be absolutely certain that it really was epilepsy all the time? Many doubts arise and Cawthorne seems to be in the right when he remarks:

'Plutarch, writing in Greek, refers to this as *Epileptikois*, a term used in those days for any seizure that caused the sufferers to fall down and be helpless. It is not surprising that many writers translated this as epilepsy, and so the term 'falling sickness' and epilepsy have been loosely regarded as the same thing. Suetonius, writing in Latin, uses the term *morbus comitialis*, the disease which, when it attacked a member of a committee, ended the meeting. Clearly such a description could include epilepsy, a stroke, a heart attack and also an attack of Meniere's disease.'[1]

Morbus comitialis must have been a patently broader category and would not merely have included epilepsy – not because of a deliberate 'classificatory' choice by the ancients (physicians and superstitious alike) but simply because they were unable to distinguish between similarly presenting conditions. In addition, Plutarch, as Cawthorne suggests, may even have used *epileptikois* in a broader sense, just as is the case with *morbus comitialis*. Yet, even assuming that by 'epileptic fits' Plutarch really meant a typical epileptic presentation and, considering he was consulting Latin sources, is it not possible that he misunderstood the exact meaning of the words found in original accounts like that of Gaius Oppius?[2] The concept of *morbus comitialis*, a disease interrupting a public assembly, was alien to him as nothing of the sort existed in Greece. May it not be that he, in reading *morbus comitialis* and grasping for meaning, understood it in a way closest to a similar concept in his native language? Plutarch's knowledge and use of his sources is exceptional, nevertheless he himself wrote that his knowledge of the Latin language was not very good. He only knew as much as was necessary to him to follow the facts and stories he found in Roman archives and libraries since he was already familiar with the facts and course of events. Yet, as he admitted, he believed that if one learns a foreign language as an adult one is unable to learn the subtleties of it, a task that better suits a younger person.[3] Undoubtedly, as Antonio La Penna remarks,[4] Plutarch must have had aids and translators, yet to master linguistic subtleties and notions of a foreign language always offers a better understanding of the culture and dynamics of an alien country than relying on the help of interpreters. Thus, the possibility that the Greek attributed *morbus comitialis* a stronger purely epileptic interpretation should be considered. This scenario seems more likely than Cawthorne's, in which *morbus comitialis* and *epileptikois* are both very general definitions, although one that is also worth considering.

The Roman poet Lucretius left us a wonderful description of a typical epileptic attack, stressing the eye-catching symptoms and presentation:

'Often will someone in a sudden fit, As if by stroke of lightning, tumble down Before our eyes, and sputter foam, and grunt, Blither, and twist about with sinews taut, Gasp up in starts, and weary out his limbs With tossing round.'[5]

Why is there no such description pertaining to Julius Caesar and, on the contrary why are the symptoms recorded so much vaguer and milder? In any man of his rank, constantly in the public spotlight, some more episodes and at least one or two episodes like the one versified by Lucretius should be present and yet there is nothing of the sort. From this it can be inferred that the 'fits', headaches and other psychomotor symptoms which have been called epilepsy/*morbus comitialis* may well have been something else and that other alternative diagnoses should be considered.

Having discarded most of the theories, we are left with one which, more logically and in a simpler way than the others, would explain:

a. his familial background highly suggestive of cardiovascular/cerebrovascular disease (heart attack, lethal stroke);
b. all of his symptoms including the mood and personality changes of his late phase and their milder presentation;
c. the absence of clear descriptions of typical epileptic attacks;

d. the confusion with epilepsy given a certain resemblance of symptoms, especially falls/fits.

The answer we have put forward is cerebrovascular disease in the form of multiple mini strokes, also known as transient ischemic attacks (TIAs), which, unlike full-blown strokes (which could have left him severely impaired and with grave cognitive deficits), would very much describe his vague symptomatology and the repeated presentation. TIAs occur when arteries of the cerebral circulation become occluded, thus oxygen delivery to neurons is suspended, resulting in focal neurological deficits. Unlike stroke, however, TIAs resolve much more rapidly (from minutes to a maximum 24 hours) and leave less severe consequences. All cerebrovascular diseases tend to increase progressively in frequency after fifty years of age and Caesar was likely already 51-years old when they started, an age much higher than the average life expectancy (25 years) in a population where only 25 per cent of people were aged over 40-years. Risk factors for TIAs, as well as for strokes, would have included aortic hypertension, diabetes, lipid-rich diet, obesity but also cardiac pathologies such as atrial fibrillation, aortic or mitral valve disease, myocardial infarction, embolus, arteritis, migraine, vertebral osteophytes compressing the vertebral artery and so on.[6] Speculating on the exact etiology of these TIAs would be too much since the symptoms reported in the sources do not allow us to go any further from semiology and identification of the system involved (cardiovascular) and its most likely mechanism (TIAs rather than massive haemorrhage or stroke). Although Caesar's diet was possibly sparse (either from military campaigns or comprising low cardiovascular risk through the Roman ancestor of what is now known as the 'Mediterranean Diet', which at the time would include fish and seafood, vegetables, oil, wine and bread),[7] it may also have been rich and opulent as he was a powerful politician-general, so that identifying the exact breakdown of inherited versus environmental components of his atherosclerotic load is challenging. As a consequence it is equally difficult to speculate as to whether any cardiovascular events derived from cardiac embolization or from atherosclerotic plaques, but what is clear is that he was a middle-aged Caucasian without the benefits of modern day cholesterol-lowering medications and had possible exposure to high caloric lipid laden foods whilst also adhering to the aerobic cardiovascular fitness needs of a consistently successful Roman general. In spite of these hypotheses about his diet, however, the sources suggest that his was more likely to be a moderate one.[8]

The issue of cerebrovascular disease could also account for Caesar's psychiatric type symptoms such as his emotional lability during Cicero's oration. Cerebrovascular attacks have a longstanding association with severe and chronic depressive disorders, emotionalism, affective lability and apathy. Such diseases derive from two broad components (i) awareness of current and impending neurological impairment as a result of vascular events and (ii) areas of ischaemia and infarcts corresponding to anatomical areas associated with these such as white matter gliosis and deep nuclei lacunes. In actuality, post-stroke conditions can also include dementia, mania compulsions and psychosis though these are less common. Whilst a diagnosis of epilepsy also carries a psychopathological burden, typically depression (though not as prominent and frequent as in stroke), anxiety, suicidal ideation and psychosis, these do not reflect Caesar's condition as much as those associated with cerebrovascular disease.

Such being the evidence, we are strongly persuaded that this simpler cerebrovascular explanation would fit Caesar's symptoms much better, thus providing a complete mechanism for his pathology and behaviour at the end of his life.

Could this disease have played any role in his death by assassination? Could his changing behaviour and personality, mixed with his growing desire to become king and suppress the republican institutions, have prompted his murderers to act more decidedly or more swiftly? Certainly his behaviour and declining health would have meant something to the people who plotted to get rid of him. The fact that Suetonius reports that towards the end of his life he gave the impression of being tired of life strongly points to a form of depression affecting him which, we believe, might not only be caused by his unsatisfied monarchical dream and by the provocations of his political enemies, but also by a background pathological condition. Mini strokes would not leave him with dementia or paralysed, yet his mood would have changed and that patent depression or dark mood could well have meant that he felt his time had come and he was ready to accept his fate, as beautifully depicted by Dio Cassius in the scene in which he described the image of Caesar that falls to the ground and breaks as a bad omen. Garfano and Bursztajn in 2004[9] put forward the idea that Caesar, suffering from depression and such problems – they thought caused by temporal lobe epilepsy – decided to bring on his own death by provoking the conspirators, setting the date of his departure for the war against the Parthians so that they felt pressured to kill him. By doing this he would automatically achieve immortality as a god and put all his enemies in the terrible position of having killed an unarmed man in a weapon-free area, the Senate, thus causing the people to hate them and finally leave the republic to men of his own party, namely Octavian, his adoptive son. This thesis is a little extreme, yet like ours stresses the influence of disease on his last months and days.

Concerning Feedback from Proponents of other Theories
When novel hypotheses are presented, different kinds of reactions may ensue. Most of them, no matter their overall judgement on others' ideas, help science progress, since only by highlighting weaknesses and strengths in one's propositions is a better understanding on natural and historical phenomena achieved. In pathography and paleopathology, the possibility of sharing one's views with colleagues and liaising with specialists from different fields permits a virtuous cooperation between traditionally separate expertises. As the article emerged, we had the unique possibility to have our theory discussed on a large scale, thus getting powerful feedback from leaders in the field of classics and of medicine. Their contributions influenced the subsequent development of our research, broadening its scope and breadth and making it a richer study. In all honesty, we confess that we found most reactions in those days remarkable in terms of the openness of thought, the delicacy in presentation, the constructiveness and the respectful engagement. They greatly contributed to the debate and have positively influenced our understanding of the matter. We shall now take a look at a couple of those responses and discuss the points that emerged since scientists' aim is to advance knowledge by questioning everything – even long received tenets. With respect to this and as a disclaimer, we use the word 'scientists' in its broadest sense: from the Latin *Scientia* (knowledge), perfectly represented in modern languages by the German term *Wissenschaft*. We regard scientists as being all scholars genuinely interested in

the beauty and mystery of the world and endowed with an open mind who study nature, no matter whether chemically, biologically, historically, medically or philosophically. Scientists, in general, as the learned evolutionary biologist Professor Richard C Dawkins often reiterates, are glad to be proven wrong since that means significant advances in knowledge and education. When we proposed this new theory on Caesar's disease we were confident our medical colleagues would be interested in the debate and would find the study relevant, nevertheless we were not sure classicists would regard it as a key point in the discussion on Julius Caesar. Without proper feedback from them, we feared the study would live on purely as a medical question and the scope of the study could not be expanded.

Commenting on our theory in *El Pais*,[10] McLachlan, while defending his views on epilepsy and suggesting that nobody would ever be able to prove one theory or another (ie because Caesar's body and more data in the sources is missing), yet he underlined that epilepsy can also be caused by a stroke. By doing this he recognised the cerebrovascular possibility, at least hypothetically, which he had categorically ruled out, along with head trauma, in his 2009 study mainly focusing on dementia (absent in Caesar's case). He then remarked that in his view risk factors traditionally associated with stroke development and very common in our time, may not have been so widespread in antiquity. Specifically to this, we reply that:

a. The fact that **cardiovascular diseases are mainly a product of modern western diets and sedentary life styles** (together with a dramatic decrease in infectious-disease related deaths) has been a long-held dogma in medical education, nevertheless the scientific study of mummies (mainly Egyptian ones) has **unquestionably demonstrated this to be a wrong assumption**. There is hard evidence of the existence of such pathologies in ancient times, particularly affecting members of the upper class. Caesar was not particular about food and led a very active life, yet it is very doubtful that he was totally unexposed to the risks caused by his highly stressful endeavours. To lay it down in layman's terms and to make a comparison with the modern world, his 'job' combined the occupations of a prime minister/president, an army general, a field soldier and much more;

b. **Ictal pathology was very well recorded in antiquity**, thus it was not an uncommon clinical possibility, be it in the form of full-blown stroke or of TIAs, the latter possibly falling into the category of *morbus comitialis*;
c. As highlighted in Chapter Two, the sources may be scant, yet they say quite a lot about a potential cardiovascular and cerebrovascular disease, in particular the **familial background** points in that direction.

All in all, MacLachlan's intervention in the discussion, which we very much appreciated, albeit in *nuce*, started providing theoretical background for a new school of thought about Caesar's disease which we have witnessed growing since our theory appeared.

Some weeks after the theory had started being discussed, our study was covered in *Forbes Magazine*[11] and feedback was given by Professor Strauss who had also been doing some research on Caesar's disease as part of his book on the assassination of the dictator. His and Professor Bazil's contribution to the study of Caesar's disease have been highlighted when discussing the potential episode of *morbus comitialis* (epilepsy to them, mini strokes to us) the night before his murder and we have also already examined his hypothesis about head trauma causing secondary epilepsy. In this section we aim to analyse the theoretical outcomes and future developments his positions have produced. While he affirmed to be inclined to favour the epileptic theory, he said that the idea that, in the end, Caesar might have both cerebrovascular pathology and epilepsy caused by the former of the two could also be considered. This proved a substantial step forward in the debate on the disease of Julius Caesar. As we have remarked several times so far, when reassessing the history of characters of the past for signs of disease, caution should be the rule. Indeed, we concur that late onset epilepsy may be caused by vascular insults to the brain, since the areas that suffer ischaemia and necrosis (cellular death) may end up constituting epileptic foci, areas of the brain where communication between neurons is severely impaired and epilepsy can originate. If Caesar had a full-blown stroke, it would be a more likely possibility, since even in modern times the numbers of patients showing epileptic activity either as a presenting feature or as a sequela of a stroke is relevant, in particular considering the aging population of our times. The problem with a full blown stroke, however, is that the symptoms reported in the sources appear to be of a milder form – which is also important to remember when suggesting *grand mal* epilepsy – and if Caesar had suffered from it, then cognitive decline would have been a much more likely eventuality. The possibility of a full blown stroke may perhaps be considered when reassessing what happened between March 14 and 15. If it really was a manifestation of disease, then, considering the general confusion in which he found himself in the morning of 15 March and the facility – in spite of the fact that Caesar trusted him – with which Decimus Brutus manipulated him and took him to the Senate House, a full-blown stroke may also be cautiously considered. Nevertheless, given the fact that he did not show any major signs of it, a mini-stroke (transient ischemic attack) seems again to us a much likelier eventuality. In any case, had that been a full blown stroke, it would have been too late for him to develop epilepsy since the conspirators' dagger would not have given his necrotic cells time to produce impairment of brain electric transmissions. Thapsus remains a very interesting possibility but even there mini strokes would better explain his not too greatly impaired post eventum conditions. If TIAs were instead the explanation for his *morbus comitialis*, epilepsy could still result but even in our time definitive data on its frequency in such cases is missing – 1.8 to 3.7 per cent of frequency being one of the proposed statistics.[12] In addition, a transient ischemic attack may sometimes be confused with a focal seizure, such as limb-shaking ones, so the possibility that Caesar first had mini-strokes that eventually caused him to develop focal seizures which may still present in a fashion not too dissimilar from TIAs should not be discarded.[13] This last reflection leads us to the following conclusions:

a. once more it should be stressed that *morbus comitialis* was not purely epilepsy and that other pathological entities mimicking it could well fall into the category;

b. if one really wants to maintain that he was epileptic, then focal seizures, causing lower-grade and less eye-catching manifestations, seem to be the more likely possibility;

c. on account of the description by Pliny and of clinical likelihood, it does seem in any case more probable that, if he really had both, TIAs came first and were present for a longer time.

More or less in the same period, Montemurro and colleagues (2015)[14] presented their theory that Caesar might have had arteriovenous malformation, which followed in the footsteps of our study. However, they still insisted on preserving the epileptic part of the story. As for cerebrovascular attacks, epilepsy would be a possibility. While we personally believe that Caesar only had mini strokes, such new ideas have represented a major shift from earlier views about Caesar's epilepsy. Until then, with the exception of Kanngiesser who spoke of *epilepsia senile* caused by atherosclerosis, cardiovascular and cerebrovascular diseases had largely been ignored and the story had been but a table-tennis etiological match between *inherited-early-onset-epilepsy-embracing-the-whole-of-the-Julio-Claudian clan* and *late onset-epilepsy-the-quest-for-the-most-complicated-cause*, rarely interspersed with semiological 'breaks' between supporters of '*grand mal* typical presentation of epilepsy' and '*petit mal* epilepsy'. The sources are scant and we certainly respect the views of those who support the epileptic theory, but we must confess to be very pleased to have, in any case, caused the focus to shift to the Julian family and the cardiovascular disease likely present in generations before Caesar. This is the direction in which future studies, pro-epilepsy or contra-epilepsy, should go. Looking for hyper-complicated trees of epilepsy and trying to prove Caesar's alleged epilepsy through Caligula or Nero, or reading his ancestors' deaths in terms of SUDEP are unlikely to clarify the nature of Caesar's pathology.

As we were being interviewed by the well-documented (no *captatio benevolentiae* intended!) Miguel A Criado from *El Pais*, one question particularly caught our attention, namely if we thought that, no matter the weight of our evidence for our newly proposed theory, no matter the likelihood of a cardiovascular disease in his family, no matter the issues we highlighted in other stances, in people's minds Caesar will always be considered epileptic. The question also continued by asking whether we thought Shakespeare had any role in the establishment of this perception.

Our view is that once historical characters enter the dimension of myth most of their attributes become deformed until the man is hardly distinguishable from the marble statue he has turned into. Caesar knew this perfectly well, he knew what epilepsy really meant in people's minds and the fact that after two thousand years the conundrum of his health is still fiercely debated and that an aura of myth surrounds his illness putting him on a par with other famous historical conquerors proves he was right. Shakespeare's immortal verses have undoubtedly shaped our perception and it's no surprise that notions such as 'the falling sickness', a higher number of stab wounds, the foam at the mouth and many more details of the like still generate confusion simply by the power of their symbolism. Mini strokes, cerebrovascular disease in general, may seem too-human diseases, evidence of older age and progressive, albeit not catastrophic decline. To separate history from myth, however, is the historian's and, in this particular case, the physician's duty.

As his body lay lifeless on the ground of Pompey's Curia, as the French historian Michelet remarked,[15] Caesar had never been so powerful. His death caused the empire to be born and his name became godly and immortal. His disease undoubtedly had an impact during his last years, months and days and people around him must have noticed it. To say that this alone, or primarily this, had caused the plotters to fix the time of his assassination or even to summon the courage to make that final step and take his life would be a step too far. Nonetheless, as bad omens, prophecies, auspices, strange occurrences and many more peculiar details are so often and abundantly cited when determining the sequence of Caesar's final hours and speculation is made over their significance and symbolic value, we believe that medical data, blurred as they are, should be equally taken into account, since they influence an individual's life and being rooted in biology observe its laws and, unlike omens, can to a certain extent be predicted in their outcomes.

We have remarked that Caesar's health is still debated and we have said that he knew the real power of myth and the aura surrounding epilepsy. A question, leading us to the final chapter of this book, then arises: could he, or somebody around him, have a vested interest in the existence of such confusion? Could this explain why, besides Shakespeare, the epileptic theory has so far been so successful in convincing people?

Chapter Five

Why Has the Epileptic Theory Been So Successful?

We have come to the end of our journey through the disease and its political consequences for one of history's greatest sons. We have examined the last evidence about Caesar's body, following the conspirators' stabs, that took the last breath of life from him, and lamented the loss of fundamental palaeopathological information on his assassination and disease that ensued from the burning of his body on the pyre. We have consulted the original sources, quoting the phrases where the primary evidence for such a disease, or even the subtlest physical and potentially pathological details, is mentioned, explaining them in depth in order to give our readers a complete overview of how much is really known about Caesar's sufferings and, above all, how much of it can actually be found in the ancient texts and is not some later reinterpretation, grounded in logical sequiturs, intuitions or even mere speculations. We have seen how this evidence is scant and simply not clear enough to decree that he was an epileptic. We have highlighted the contradictions and weaknesses in the decisive passages and questioned the foundations of the epileptic assumption. We have examined how theories accepting epilepsy may suffer from serious historical and philological limitations, reducing their number to a few, a great part of which converge with the general background of cardiovascular pathology and specifically cerebrovascular disease that our own theory implies. We have rediscovered and analysed old medical and historical literature which attempted to dismantle the epileptic theory questioning in different ways its foundations, nonetheless underlining the mistakes their proponents have made both in providing unlikely differential diagnoses and in suggesting (two out of three) that Caesar had no disease at the end of his life at all. At the same time we have explained how a major disease like cancer or a progressive degenerative disease is just as unlikely as that theory. We have then put forward our idea that mini strokes would explain the patently genetic pathological cardiovascular background, suggested by the reference to his ancestors' deaths found in Pliny, and his manifestations, from falls, to dizziness and psychomotor changes. We have, moreover, remarked how this theory is much simpler, does without unnecessary complications and speculative assertions, and, unlike the others, is very balanced and cautious at the same time. We have also discussed reactions to our proposal of the new theory and answered the points raised by them.

One major question has not been formulated and answered yet. It will not be easy to do both, thus we will endeavour to do it as schematically as possible.

a. If epilepsy happened to be confused with other diseases involving a somewhat similar spectrum of symptoms;

And

b. epilepsy was considered a curse sent by the gods, a stigma one would have to bear for the rest of one's life;

And

c. if we say that Caesar did not suffer from epilepsy;

Why then has this confusion been possible, and above all, allowed to persist? Indeed, a broader meaning of the expression *morbus comitialis* and a Greek's (Plutarch's) limited understanding of the subtleties of the Latin language and of the very notion of such an illness may well, as we argued at length, have contributed to the situation, but what was the purpose of such confusion? Why was clarity on the matter never made in ancient times? These interrogatives ensue:

i. If it really was epilepsy and there was no way to hide it, why was it not stated in clearer terms, described fully and with abundance of details as one would expect?

ii. On the contrary, why if it was not epilepsy as we are persuaded is actually the case, does such a confusion exist, involving a disease most authorities in classical scholarships would define a curse?

iii. Why, finally, if one looks at epilepsy as a supernaturally empowering condition as some in nineteenth century tried to stress, was it not treated as in i.?

Such points are of the utmost importance and, given the highly politicized context in which Caesar's disease occurred, the answers, we believe, must lie within the very actors on the stage of that glorious tragedy that defined the fate of the Roman Republic, turning it into arguably the greatest empire of all time. These actors are: the plotters, Julius Caesar himself and his legal successor Octavian. We now aim to examine their motivations and the likelihood of various scenarios. We specify that this three-fold synthesis does not necessarily mean that only, and exclusively, one of them took place. Although the actors involved may have had different goals, contamination or involuntary interaction between the three is certainly a possibility that ought not to be ignored. Because of this, we kindly invite the readers to think of this arrangement of the matter as a simplification meant to disentangle a highly complex puzzle, a conundrum by no means inferior in complexity and traps to that of the nature of Caesar's disease.

The Plotters
Killing Caesar was a risky decision, not only because of the obvious difficulty in carrying out the plan, but also because of the general uncertainty about the aftermath. In their view, Caesar's proverbial sexual and political appetites had turned violent and predatory, moving from women, riches and foreign lands ultimately to the very heart of their world, Rome, the capital of what was then the sole western and eastern superpower. He had marched against his Fatherland, slaughtered its sons and brave soldiers who had sworn their loyalty to it simply to make his name and his power greater and greater. They thought he had raped the Republic turning her into his concubine and making her customs nothing more than a lurid bunch of unnecessary dusty decrees he could hardly bear and would soon substitute with his sole will and word. Every act, every word by him expressed his total disregard of law.

The often quoted Suetonius gives us one more story, which really says it all about the dictator's ambitions:

> 'Some think that habit had given him a love of power, and that weighing the strength of his adversaries against his own, he grasped the opportunity of usurping the despotism which had been his heart's desire from early youth'.

Cicero too was seemingly of this opinion, when he wrote in the third book of his *De Officiis* that Caesar ever had upon his lips these lines of Euripides, of which Cicero himself adds a version:

> 'If wrong may e'er be right, for a throne's sake
> Were wrong most right:— be God in all else feared.'[1]

This was the man had become now their master, a man who had sacrificed liberty and Rome on the very altar of his ego. They just could not tolerate this and such rhetoric must have inflamed their secret meetings and feverish planning. They knew they had to act, but how and when? Caesar's ambition and lust for conquest had crushed anyone who had dared to stand in his way and no armies were left to defend the legitimate republican order from the passions and goals of the monster. If anything was to be done, it would be their duty. They deluded themselves into believing that by killing Caesar the state and its freedom would be regained, that the people would acclaim them as liberators, as heroes, as the ancient Brutus had been acclaimed when he expelled the last king from the city walls. We said it was a risky decision. Indeed, it was. Removing Caesar would mean leaving a power vacuum which they had to make sure other 'monsters', other would-be tyrants, namely the dictator's associates such as Mark Antony, would not fill. It was a very dangerous move, but they had to act. Even though in the depths of their hearts they hoped that the people of Rome would salute them as those who had freed them from the yoke of Caesarian servitude, they were not so naive as to expect this would happen automatically. For Roman noblemen liberty was the highest value in life, something to live and die for. It meant political power and connection with a glorious tradition, the *mos maiorum*, the customs and institutions inherited from their ancestors. For the ordinary plebeian – and Rome crawled with them – stuffing his stomach with a loaf of bread or distracting himself with gladiatorial spectacles or chariot races was something more practical, closer to everyday life than the destiny of the Republic. The old rule *panem et circenses*, was (and probably still is) the key to taming the masses. Caesar knew this perfectly well and excelled in giving the mob what they wanted. His donations would win him the love of the Roman crowd. The conspirators must have seen in this an example of the old seducer in action: with the same nonchalance with which he took his pleasures from countless women, he seduced the common man, who, because of poverty, would sell his right to defend the Republican institutions for the mentioned loaf of bread and some drops of blood poured onto the sand of the arena. This being the situation, the plotters needed a shift in perception. They started spreading the idea (maybe even true) that Caesar was about to renounce his life dictatorship to proclaim himself king, that the long-banned monarchy would soon return to Rome, or that it had already returned. The very definition 'tyrant' was being used more and more. The effect of this would be strictly limited and Caesar's will, made public following his assassination, in which he left his money to the people of Rome, overturned it. Anger exploded and the conspirators were forced to flee like vulgar assassins: in the eyes of the common man they had but vilely slaughtered their benefactor and leader, the man who had won them supremacy in Gaul, Britannia, Egypt, and Africa. He had fooled them again, even in death; the Republic would never be reborn and the rest of Rome's history would unfold as a struggle for power between militarily-supported empire-aspiring factions.

Is it possible that Caesar's disease played any role at all in this scenario? Following in the footsteps of the Garofano-Bursztajn study,[2] but much more cautiously, we have suggested the idea that Caesar understood that his health was declining, especially from a psychomotor point of view, and that, rather fatalistically, he accepted his downfall – be it in the sandy expanses of Persia or in the Roman Curia, at the hands of a Parthian or at those of his countrymen – which would have meant for him going beyond the hardly achievable title of king, straightforwardly obtaining divine status, something which would put him on a par with Hercules and Alexander the Great. In his judgement his mortal path had come to an end – it would have been hard for him to achieve much more than he had already won for himself – but he could become a god, sacrificed by evil plotters who had betrayed his trust and forgiveness and who put – in his view – their political ambitions before the well-being of the Roman people and the general peace of the state. Specifically focusing on the plotters' reactions to his declining health conditions, we explained how these might have influenced their timing, as much as the episodes involving his rebuttal of offers of crowns or excessive honours. To say that this alone caused them to plan the assassination would be what we have called an attempt to 'biologize' history, making a disease responsible for the course of important events, when in fact several factors contributed in varying proportions. We certainly reject that *in toto* as an approach.[3] Now, how would calling Caesar an epileptic have influenced their actions and plans? Two possibilities can be examined:

i. **Epilepsy as a curse.** In the sources no mention is made of the conspirators speaking of Caesar's alleged epilepsy. Surely, if they viewed it as a curse, they would have found more moral justifications for their act, so why then not stress it more, linking it to the hammering underground propaganda that Caesar was a tyrant? Calling him an epileptic tyrant, would have meant 'the despot cursed by the gods who will bring our state to destruction'. Did they instead view epilepsy in the light of a supposedly positive connection with the divine sphere? Or did they just see things for what they probably were, namely that Caesar fell, had certain problems, his health was decaying but that his was not a typical case of epilepsy? The last hypothesis clearly finds our support but we should also make a political remark: would killing a sick old man really make them look like heroes and liberators?[4]

ii. **Epilepsy as an empowering condition.** As a logical consequence to the last rhetorical question, it can be speculated that Caesar's condition was deteriorating, thus the plotters were influenced to act. Calling him an epileptic would probably have helped their propaganda move to depict him as the very curse sent from the gods but:
   - the evidence, visual and reported, just did not support this claim enough, so people would not believe it;

- Instead of playing the 'cursed by the gods' card, they could play another card, the 'divinity-aspiring' one, thus remarking his arrogance and ambitions to create a divine-right-style monarchy. This would mean that they were killing a powerfully dangerous man, not a weakened old lion. Why did they not do that? They actually did, but primarily in political terms, since the political acts were much more convincing than his undefined disease, likely of cerebrovascular origin as we posit, vaguely resembling epilepsy but not enough to allow either propaganda moves.

In summary, the plotters' failure to mention his disease stems from their desire to make the people think they were killing a strong and evil man. Their failure to call him epileptic can be explained by the dual nature of the aura surrounding that disease, which would not necessarily help their plan and above all the unconvincing visual evidence that his falls were really symptoms of epileptic attacks. For these reasons, we reject the idea that they had any part in the survival, spreading and ultimate historical success of the epileptic theory.

The *prima donna*, Julius Caesar himself
We concluded our 2015 neurological article with the following words:

> 'Caesar and his adopted son Octavius may have contributed to the diagnosis of epilepsy, as this was considered a "sacred disease" so that they would have publicised this disorder to better fit with Caesar's public profile.'[5]

Coming back to the methodological points we highlighted in Chapter Four, it is important to remark that even in that short piece the core of the present chapter could be found. We finally have the opportunity to explain them fully, separating Caesar from Octavian, although in the article we made it a clear point that we should look at them as a whole, since the latter's success inevitably stemmed from the former's success and aura of divinity. As we discussed in Chapters Three and Four, different interpretations of epilepsy are present, although it is generally accepted that it was perceived as a curse sent from the gods. This was certainly the meaning it had in classical Greece as a general rule, yet, when present in prominent men, a more cautious approach ought to be adopted. Naively endorsing nineteenth-century Lombrosian views on genius and epilepsy to explain the treated subject – obviously only for the sake of contextualizing historical notions of disease – may be one step too far, as is too hurriedly conflating notions of enthusiasm, that is the divine possession, or mania, capable of inspiring priestesses such as those of Pythian Apollo, or men of profound philosophical enquiry, like Socrates, with psychiatric conditions. Nevertheless, one would be equally far from the truth if one were of the opinion that such ideas, in particular the epilepsy-genius link, were the mere product of the century of phrenology, racial anthropology, craniometry and of the first, shy steps, still permeated by philosophy and to some extent religion, taken by that new discipline called psychiatry. Such ideas were only reinterpreted and presented in a new fashion, moulded so that they could be everlasting theories capable of explaining the achievements of men of success in purely, or at least primarily, biological terms. The genius was such because of his abnormality, which could be explained in neuropsychiatric terms: he suffered from an incapacitating condition known as epilepsy, but this very defect had somehow shaped the neuroanatomical and chemical architecture producing his intelligence in a manner that made his brilliance manifest. His sufferings, defects, alienation from friendships and society, melancholic solitude were balanced by superhuman qualities, which allowed him to stand out from the *vulgus*, the dull and amorphous mass of ordinary men unrecorded by history mere instruments in the hands of these greater men's will. Such superhuman properties, linked them to the divine sphere, conferring upon them the aura of sacredness and inspiring reverence and devotion. We do not exactly know if poets of old suffered or were reported to suffer from epilepsy or epilepsy-resembling conditions, but the very concept that a poetic mania, an obsession filling their mortal bodies and exciting their immortal souls, of a – as Plato suggests in several of his dialogues – divine nature, is endemic in classical antiquity and its influences would be and perhaps still are – seen for many a century to ensue. As brilliantly remarked in recent times, two passages, the first by Plutarch and the second by Cicero deserves great attention.

In his *Life of Lysander*, Plutarch describes the virtues and alleged psychiatric condition affecting the Spartan admiral (died 395 BC) who crushed Athens during the Peloponnesian War (431–405 BC):

> 'The **father of Lysander**, Aristocleitus, is said to have been **of the lineage of the Heracleidae**, though not of the royal family. But Lysander was reared in poverty, and showed himself as much as any man conformable to the customs of his people; of a manly spirit, too, and superior to every pleasure, excepting only that which their good deeds bring to those who are successful and honoured. To this pleasure it is no disgrace for the youth in Sparta to succumb. [...] But he seems to have been naturally subservient to men of power and influence, beyond what was usual in a Spartan, and content to endure an arrogant authority for the sake of gaining his ends, a trait which some hold to be no small part of political ability. And **Aristotle**, when he sets forth that **great natures, like those of Socrates and Plato and Heracles, have a tendency to melancholy**, writes also that **Lysander, not immediately, but when well on in years, was a prey to melancholy.**'[6]

This quotation is of paramount importance since it highlights exactly what we were arguing a moment ago: abnormal mental conditions were already linked to greatness in ancient times and a direct reference is made to the works of Aristotle of Stagira (384–322 BC). Melancholy, or melancholia, (literally 'black bile') has a long history and finds its origins in the humoral theory developed by ancient Greek physicians, according to which the combinations of the four basic humors (black bile, yellow bile, phlegm and blood) determined an individual's character and mood. Melancholy specifically defined a touch of sadness pervading one's character, pushing a person to deep introspection and a feeling of impotence, not too far from a condition of depression. Depression is found in epileptics, so we'll shortly come back to this as well as to the other highlighted reference, at the beginning of the paragraph, to Lysander's alleged descent from Hercules, whom the Romans called Heracles. It may just be a trivial claim Plutarch made, yet it is relevant to our discussion.

The second passage is a very concise reference found in Cicero's *Tuscolanae Disputationes*:

> 'Aristotle, indeed, says that **all men of genius are melancholic** [*omnis ingeniosos melancholicos esse*]; so that I should be sad about being more dim-witted than I really am. He lists **many** [*enumerat multos*], as if there were a fact, brings his arguments why it be so.'[7]

Again, a reference to a passage in Aristotle's works is made and melancholy is cited again as associated with genius. Cicero also says that many people presenting that association are listed by Aristotle to prove his point, which he treats as a fact, not as a mere hypothesis. Such an approach may be defined as unscientific in the modern acceptation of the term, and we certainly concur, since evidence is to be produced by means of biological data and experiments, yet it is somewhat striking, from Cicero's words, to see that Aristotle's means of giving reasons for the pathology-greatness link is not too different from Lombroso's, who would but provide a longer list of men and references to the 'sciences' of his times – craniometry, phrenology and behavioural assumptions and debatable observations instead of the complex blending of basic humors – thus turning what the ancient author epitomised in one paragraph into a full book, the already mentioned *The Man of Genius*.

Let us now take a closer look at the passage to which Plutarch and Cicero allude, specifying that it comes from the *Problemata* (Problems), a work alternatively attributed to Aristotle or – more likely – defined as written by Pseudo-Aristotle. In any case it came from the Peripatetic School, a philosophical movement founded by Aristotle of Stagira, and is a collection of problems which kept being enriched for several centuries through until the end of the classical world.

> 'WHY is it that **all those who have become eminent in philosophy or politics or poetry or the arts are clearly of an atrabilious temperament** [literal Greek: μελανγχολικοὶ ὄντες, *melangcholikoì óntes*, being melancholic, hence their mood/character being influenced by black/dark bile], and some of them to such an extent as to **be affected by diseases caused by black bile**, as is said to have happened

to **Heracles among the heroes?** For he appears to have been of this nature, wherefore **epileptic afflictions** were **called by the ancients the sacred disease** [Greek: ἱεράν νόσον, *hieràn nóson*] **after him**. That his temperament was **atrabilious** is shown by the **fury** which he **displayed towards his children and the eruption of sores** which took place before his disappearance on Mount Oeta; for this often occurs as the result of black bile. **Lysander the Lacedaemonian also suffered from similar sores before his death.** There are also the stories of **Ajax and Bellerophon,** of whom the former **became insane** [ἐκστατικός, *ekstaticós, ecstatic*], while the latter sought out **habitations in desert places.**

'And many others of the heroes seem to have been similarly afflicted, and among men **of recent times Empedocles, Plato, and Socrates, and numerous other well-known men,** and also **most of the poets.** For many such persons have bodily afflictions as the result of this kind of temperament, while some of them obviously possess a natural inclination to affections of this kind; in a word, they all, as has been said, are naturally atrabilious. The cause of this may be understood if we first take an example from **the effect of wine, which if taken in large quantities appears to produce such qualities as we attribute to the atrabilious,** inducing, as it is drunk, many different characteristics, making men for instance **irritable, benevolent, compassionate, or reckless;** whereas no such results are produced by honey or milk or water or anything similar. One can easily see that wine has a variety of effects by observing how it gradually changes those who drink it for, finding them **chilled and taciturn as the result of abstinence, a small quantity makes them more talkative, while a larger quantity makes them eloquent and bold, and, when they proceed to action, reckless, and a still larger quantity makes them insolent and afterwards frenzied,** while outrageous excess enfeebles them and makes them **stupid like those who have been epileptic from childhood,** and very similar to those who are exceedingly atrabilious.'[8]

This passage is an eye-opening one, no matter what one's stance on the topic may be. The ancients, at least some of them, had established a causal link between black bile and a certain type of character which was shared by most great men, both from mythology and from recorded history. It goes, however, way further in stating that:

a. Melancholy and epilepsy are linked, since Heracles the demi-godly hero was melancholic of temperament and is said to have suffered from epileptic fits. It is not so easy to determine whence the epilepsy story was derived. One hypothesis is that it comes from Euripides' (the last of the three major Greek playwrights, c.480–406 BC) and his play *The Madness of Heracles*[9] (Latin *Hercules Furens*) served this function. Probably the idea had already been widespread in people's mind and orally transmitted myths for a long time by then, yet there is a concrete possibility that the play exerted a reinforcing effect in a fashion similar to the great influence had by Shakespeare's work on the idea that Julius Caesar really suffered from epilepsy. The following verses – a messenger's report – clearly describe a sudden change resulting in an episode of folly, but in strict neurological terms it has been suggested that they may show a partial-complex seizure eventually turning into a long twilight state in which the patient is unable to control his will and actions: 'Victims to purify the house were stationed before the altar of Zeus, for Heracles had slain and cast from his halls the king of the land. There stood his group of lovely children, with his sire and Megara; and already the basket was being passed round the altar, and we were keeping holy silence. But just as Alcmena's son was bringing the torch in his right hand to dip it in the holy water, he stopped without a word. And as their father lingered, his children looked at him; and lo! He was changed; his eyes were rolling; he was distraught; his eyeballs were bloodshot and starting from their sockets, and foam was oozing down his bearded cheek.'

b. epilepsy is considered as a subtype of melancholy, or part of its spectrum of manifestations;

c. since the disease affected Heracles, not an ordinary mortal, it was renamed 'sacred';

d. behavioural and mood changes, including fury, can be caused by melancholy – we could perhaps wonder whether it was depression [melancholy] or epilepsy caused this more;

e. although early onset epileptic attacks are known to the author of this treatise since he towards the end says 'stupid like those who have been epileptic from childhood', in all of the cases he mentions epilepsy/madness seems to have presented at a late stage, causing men to turn mad, act furiously or, in some cases, live secluded lives;

f. a parallel between melancholic statuses may be made with the known effects produced by a known drug, wine – a substance far different from divine mania and much more tangible, yet capable of producing similar results in mind and body.

Furthermore, when the author talks about madness, in particular, the one affecting Ajax, he uses the Greek *ekstatikós*, which can mean 'excitable, out of one's senses', an adjective derived from the word *ékstasis* (English: ecstasies), a distraction of the mind caused by powerful stimuli such as anger or fear, by alcoholic fluids (wine), or finally an entrancement, a trance possessing an individual. At the beginning of this discussion on the link between epilepsy and the divine sphere, we said that caution should be the rule when associating it or other forms of psychiatric disease with the poetic mania, the entrancement of which Plato, referring to Socrates, speaks. This is still our stance, yet it is astounding to read in this passage the constant references to poets suffering from melancholy/epilepsy/mania, the cause rather than a by-product of their greatness and semi-divine condition.

Summing the matter up, it can be said that already in antiquity epilepsy – via melancholy – had come to be associated not only with madness and terrible acts deriving from it (like Heracles' murder of his family) but also to a divine possession and connection allowing certain men to rise above the rest of mankind because of their superhuman accomplishments. Understandably, the ancients posited that there was a fine line between the expression of pure genius and horrific outbursts of fury and folly, which made this condition unique. It was undoubtedly a 'sacred' disease because the gods sent it onto men as a punishment, but also a strong connection between mortal and immortal worlds. Whilst epilepsy and depression (melancholy) must – as they nowadays do – have affected men of all social conditions and intellectual powers, it is relevant that these very diseases were uniquely affecting a handful of elite individuals, who probably – it must have been thought at the time – enjoyed greater powers on account of those ailments.

Now, such being the perception of epilepsy, how would Caesar behave as a consequence? Since he was very unlikely to have been epileptic, as we explained, would he be interested in letting the rumours live on and spread? Why so? What could he practically achieve by doing so?

Donnadieu gives his view of the facts:

> 'One supposes what advantage the dictator could take of this affliction, because of its nature. His appeal to the marvellous was extremely frequent. Before him, others had equally used mystification with the legions.'[10]

Thus, in his opinion, Caesar knew how politically important and effective the appeal to the supernatural could be in a society deeply characterised by superstition. He was aware that signs and symbols were more powerful and had a greater impact on the feeble and illiterate than dozens of scholarly argued treatises. Unlike Donnadieu, we are of the opinion that extreme consequences should not be drawn: all Caesar did was matter of fact and he was no actor, yet he knew the laws governing the human stage on which he was running the show. Used properly and with a pinch of audacity, such power of sensation could have made a wonderful psychological *Wunderwaffe* on the political field of battlefield.

Professor Luciano Canfora, in his all-encompassing biography of the dictator, has highlighted this aspect of Caesar's personality in much greater detail than anybody else, offering a superb portrait of the daredevil's ability to turn all sorts of falls (political, military or physical) into successes:

> 'Caesar had **never** taken **too seriously** the cumbrous apparatus of superstition that so obtrusively governed Roman public life. His **totally secular cast of mind** allowed him to take a detached view of those beliefs, which were **of primary importance in daily affairs**. But there was **a public aspect** to it all, **which he was able to keep**

in mind. He did not put off his departure to Africa [...] But when, on disembarking, he stumbled and fell, he turned that bad omen to good, exclaiming: '*Teneo te, Africa!*' almost as if he had thrown himself down to kiss the ground.'[11]

Canfora also gives one more example of the kind to maintain this view of Caesar's psychology. He recalls how there was a prophecy according to which noboby called Scipio could ever be defeated on African soil and that a Scipio was one of the opposing commanders. For this reason, Caesar wanted to have a lesser member of the gens Cornelia (to which the Scipiones belonged) in his camp, too.

Such a fearless and unscrupulous use of superstition as a political means to achieve and consolidate power was thus a prominent trait of his genius, a trait so marked that it led Donnadieu to formulate the radical conclusion we saw in chapter three, that Caesar pretended to be epileptic to empower himself in the eyes of his fellow Romans. Let's follow his reasoning:

'[...] Caesar's disease was known [...] by legionaries and by the public, it was important not to consider it as an ordinary disease [*il importait de ne pas la considérer comme une maladie ordinaire*]. That is to say that, on account of his political aims, Caesar could be as ill as the humblest of his legionaries and so his entourage, anticipating or satisfying the dictator's views, were led to attribute the troubles of his health to an affliction which, instead of belittling him, extolled his nature of man and made him somehow partake of that of the gods [*le faisait participer en quelque sorte à celle des dieux*]; the '*morbus comitialis*', because its symptoms, perfectly suited the political goals of the dictator, who, wanting to be God to be King, was suffering from a disease both divine and royal [*d'une maladie à la fois divine et royale*].'[12]

Donnadieu's words brilliantly dissect the dictator's mindset and the fact that his entourage may well have aided his plans, whether he told them to act so or simply expected it of them. The sole problem with Donnadieu's views is that they are so extreme in performing the equation between *morbus comitialis* and *morbus regius* [ie the royal disease]. This caused his stance to be criticised by Oliver Temkin and Terence Hughes. Temkin remarked that the earliest reference *morbus regius* was medieval, hence a long time after Caesar's day, precisely in a 1571 doctoral thesis, where Temkin thought confusion was probably made between icterus (ie jaundice) and epilepsy, the former actually being what *morbus regius* referred to.[13] Hughes likewise dismissed the link between *morbus regius* and *morbus comotialis* by quoting instead from Dr Ferdinand Hauthal's lexical note found in his nineteenth century Berlin edition of Helenius Acron's and Pomponius Porphyrion's *Commentary on the poet Quintus Horatius Flaccus* (*Acronis et Porphyrionis commentarii in Q. Horatium Flaccum*), which we report and translate here:

'*regius. Quem quidam daemoniacum, Alii comitialem, Alii arquatum uocant, quem Graeci* ἴκτερον *dicunt. Quibus oculi uirides sunt.*'

'Royal. Which some call 'demonic', others 'of the assembly', others 'arched' [ie the rainbow look of the eyes], which the Greek name ἴκτερον [íkteron, jaundice]. Whose [ie the patients suffering from it] eyes are green.'[14]

Those two remarks may rule out the likelihood of the *morbus regius* being the same as *morbus comitialis*, yet the fact that Temkin calls it doubtful and even in the reference quoted by Hughes *morbus comitialis* is given as synonym, we may well be led to believe that a certain degree of confusion existed in ancient medicine. It would be then very interesting to understand whether this confusion was created in the Middle Ages by the mixture of two completely different concepts or if it was some legacy from classical antiquity. Despite this, we have explained why epilepsy did not merely have negative – albeit undeniable – connotations; especially when attributed to great men; it could even explain their genius. For this reason denying the possibility that Caesar may have cashed in on it to achieve his political and propaganda goals simply on the feeble kinship between *morbus comitialis* and *morbus regius* appears to be an outdated argument. One may well do without it, yet being still left with the dual nature of the epileptic disease.

We must now explore the potential scenario which would have Caesar use epilepsy to his own advantage – which is what we believe to have been the more likely eventuality to have occurred. We append a couple of charming suggestions, which cannot be proved, yet which could very well fit the presented scenario.

Scenario 1: Julius Caesar has enjoyed a basically very healthy life until the end of the Gallic Wars, only suffering from the hardships of continual fighting and camp-life. As he enters the phase of the Civil Wars, being aged between 51 and 54 (49–46 BC) he starts to experience episodes of sudden loss of consciousness, dizziness, psychomotor changes, headache etc. Between 45 and 44 BC the episodes intensify, or are simply recorded better because he is not marching in some foreign land, but is under the spotlight in Rome. He realises his health is declining, especially psychologically – including the effects of great stress – and understands it is difficult to hide them. People see and record them. They see the conqueror growing older and more and more characterised by a darkening mood. The manifestations of this disease, nonetheless, are not as visually resounding as those of a typical epileptic attack. He happens to faint and tremble in public: this is not necessarily epilepsy with foam at the mouth, yet is enough to justify the definition, in some circumstances, of *'morbus comitialis'* or what has come to be known in the English language as the 'falling sickness'. Some are not convinced. The risk is that some would soon start seeing things for what they really are: he is affected with a human, very much too human disease, which testifies to his frailty and decay. Yes, he is still generally strong and works actively, yet, especially towards the end, during the last months, his psychomotor symptoms can hardly be hidden or explained merely in terms of angry reactions to potential plotters or provocations. Can one really believe that a man who has been through so much in warlike situations, who has risked losing everything at Gergovia, at Alesia, at Dyrrachium, at Munda and on each occasion has turned potential defeats into complete success, always keeping calm and in control of events, without outbursts of either rage or vengeance, asking for blood to be shed only when absolutely necessary and with a specific goal to be achieved – can one really believe that this man, over the course of a few months, would explode at some crowns put on a statue or at people calling him king? He has patently grown much more short-tempered and he cannot hide it. The presentation of his disease offers, though a credible possibility: it is vague, but has those two-to-three elements in common with epilepsy, the disease sacred and cursed at the same time. That is enough to make him consider the possibility of letting the rumour spread. Donnadieu is absolutely correct where he reflects that, Caesar being unable to conceal his medical condition, it was essential that people thought of it in terms of a divine condition that put him on a par with Hercules and hcrocs of old, figures eventually turned mad by envious gods, yet before such unfortunate epilogues, venerated champions and geniuses. This, in addition, fits his gradual deification started *intra vitam* (when he was still alive); he is gradually becoming *Divus Julius* even before those succeeding him declare it officially. Can one really be of the opinion that the master of turning defeat into victory, would have hesitated to turn his disease to his own advantage? In the end, he accepts his *Götterdämmerung*[15] and plans on his last grand campaign against the Parthians. He dismisses his guard. Whatever will happen will happen, he is ready. If it is his destiny to fall fighting enemies or civil foes, he is ready to accept this. He does not plan his death, as others have speculated, but he waits for his destiny. The man has already been fading for some time and cannot achieve much more in life; the god, the *Divus* has already been establishing himself for some time. The day he dies, he joins the number of the gods.

A Hypothetical Appendix to the Above Scenario
Could Julius Caesar have modelled his epilepsy on some of those great men of antiquity mentioned in the pseudo-Aristotelian *Problems*, or on other unmentioned famed individuals? There exist two possibilities which – speculative as they may be – are worth considering:

Hercules
We have seen how Heracles/Hercules is defined as a hero and his faculties are related to both melancholy and epilepsy. An interesting passage can be read in Suetonius:

'We also have mention of certain writings of his boyhood and early youth, such as the '**Praises of Hercules**', a tragedy 'Oedipus', and a 'Collection of Apophthegms'

It would appear that, as a young man, he developed an admiration for the figure of Heracles/Hercules to the extent of composing a poem to honour his character. How did he deal with his genius, achievements, melancholy and final episode of folly costing him the lives of his dear ones? Did he write anything about it at all? Did he cut down on the negative sides of Hercules' psychiatric symptoms, leaving only space for the glorious deeds? What specific words did he use to describe the episode? How would he comment on that famous hero's epilepsy? Unfortunately the *Praises of Hercules* [*Laudes Herculis*] no longer exist and cannot be consulted to find an answer. From the title we can only judge that the tone must have been a commendatory one: Hercules must have been one of the heroes of his youth, a model on which he could have modelled certain aspects of behaviour, at that time or even later. Suetonius then adds an interesting fact:

> '…but **Augustus forbade the publication** of all these minor works in a very brief and frank letter sent to Pompeius Macer, whom he had selected to set his libraries in order.'[16]

Why did Augustus his successor forbid the reading of those minor works? Did they contain licentious or offensive verses? Very unlikely, given the topic and type of work. Were they considered low-quality works, which were too far removed from the lapidary style of the *Commentarii* and the godly image which was conferred upon Caesar at the end of his life and eminently after his death? Did they contain critiques of power and morality, as was the style of the Greek tragedies by Euripides? Luciano Canfora expressed his view that there is no reason to believe Augustus censored them because of their low literary quality. He is rather of the opinion that they may contain some threatening allusions to turning the state upside down, to breaking the law to gain power, something that is proved by his often reiterating such quotes, a sign of his ambition to become the supreme ruler of the Roman republic. In Canfora's interpretation, Augustus took the decision that his power should not be questioned and citizens ought to be prevented from accessing such references.[17] This view has solidity, especially in the case of the tragedy *Oedipus*. We do not know in which language Caesar wrote these early works. On the one hand, had they been penned in Latin, then they could have been accessed by a wider audience of Romans; on the other hand, the elite, those interested in power (and perchance also power shift) were fluent in Greek, so had the language been Greek, it would not have been a major problem. In addition, we do not have clear information about whether Augustus exerted his power of censorship on the Greek tragedies and poems featuring Heracles or Oedipus. If their verses had any part in shaping Caesar's monarchist ambitions, his own rewriting of those works cannot have differed substantially from them, so banning them would have not meant much if the sources (the Greek texts) were still accessible by the general public. We will probably never know the reason for Augustus' action, but what if there were a sentence, or even a short allusion to his lack of belief in the superstition of his day, or the fact that he thought it unlikely that Hercules had become mad or that he was afflicted by melancholy/epilepsy? As a young man, many years before accessing the rooms of power, or maybe as he became the head of his family, his father being dead, he being hunted by Sulla, he might well have expressed his views in a much more disenchanted manner than later in life when his personal opinion on the matter might not have changed but he needed to use the power and fascination of myth and superstition to achieve his goals and, as we have put forward, turn his disease into something divine.

Alexander the Great

When discussing Alexander the Great with reference to Caesar, it must be immediately specified that throughout the latter's life the former was an obsession, a constant model and competitor. This is attested to by Plutarch:

> 'In like manner we are told again that, in Spain, when he was at leisure and was reading from the history of Alexander, he was lost in thought for a long time, and then burst into tears. His friends were astonished, and asked the reason for his tears. 'Do you not think,' said he, 'it is a matter for sorrow that while Alexander, at my age, was already king of so many peoples, I have as yet achieved no brilliant success?'[18]

The same incident is also told by Dio Cassius and Suetonius,[19] who are more detailed in saying that it occurred during his questorship, adding a few details and making some variations to the Plutarchean account. In lieu of a book about Alexander, Caesar sees a statue of Alexander in the temple of Hercules at Gades (Cádiz), but the emotional result is the same since Caesar is deeply moved.[20] As Canfora points out, Caesar himself starts a long saga of *synkrises* (comparisons) between himself and Alexander meant to decide who was the greater.[21] Since he left for Spain in 69 BC and came back hurriedly in 67 BC, at the time he was as old as Alexander when he perished, but, unlike him, Caesar had not yet subdued the known world. This would explain even better his deep sadness in beholding the statue or reading accounts of Alexander's conquests. Regarding this specific episode, Lorenzo Braccesi's reflections are very insightful, in that the scholar highlights that, while in Alexander's case his journey and deeds ended at the edge of the world in the east, Caesar's glorious path began at the opposite side of the known world, not far from Hercules' Pillars. When in Egypt with Cleopatra (48 BC), his lodgings (the Royal Palace) being in the heart of Alexandria where Alexander's mausoleum was located, it is certainly possible that he paid a visit to the great conqueror's mummified body. By that time, he had become as successful as Alexander in dominating most of the known world, although it had taken him longer, over twenty years more, to achieve his goals. The only reference to this visit is, sadly, not to be found in a historian's work, but in Marcus Annaeus Lucanus (Lucan)'s (39 – 65 AD) *Pharsalia*, a poem on the Civil War in which Caesar is portrayed as a sacrilegious blood-thirsty monster:

'And yet with brow
Dissembling fear, intrepid, through the shrines
Of Egypt's gods he strode, and round the fane
Of ancient Isis; bearing witness all
To Macedon's vigour in the days of old.
Yet did nor gold nor ornament restrain
His hasting steps, nor worship of the gods,
Nor city ramparts: but in greed of gain
He sought the cave dug out amid the tombs.
The madman offspring there of Philip lies,
The famed Pellaean robber, Fortune's friend,

Snatched off by fate, in vengeance for the world.
In sacred sepulchre the hero's limbs,
which should be scattered o'er the earth, repose,
Still spared by Fortune to these tyrant days: [...].'[22]

From this passage we understand that comparisons between the two conquerors were made both in commendatory and derogatory terms, as here where Alexander, too, is defined *illic Pellaei proles vaesana Philippi/ felix praedo, iacet* [literally 'there lies the mad offspring of Philip from Pella, Fortune's beloved robber']. As remarked above, we do not know if this incident really occurred, but we know that it is a possibility and the verses certainly inspired later re-elaborations, among which we would count the marvellous classic scene featuring actors Rex Harrison as Caesar and Elizabeth Taylor as Cleopatra in the 1963 historical epic *Cleopatra*, where the couple are seen contemplating the transparent sarcophagus where Alexander's mummy lies.

'Cleopatra: I want you to have his sword to take back with you.
Caesar: Too deeply embedded.
Cleopatra: It can be removed.
Caesar: It's buried in time.
Cleopatra: And Alexander's mantle.
Caesar: Too heavy for Caesar.
Cleopatra: His dream then. Make his dream yours, Caesar. His grand
design. Pick it up where he left off.'[23]

Caesar's desire to emulate Alexander is defined as *aemulatio Alexandri*.[24] It was a feeling that many great conquerors, following the Macedonian's demise, would share – that, no matter how great their successes Alexander would still be remembered as the greatest of all, tormented them. Some of them would imitate his gestures, his looks and his sayings. Pompey, who had already won the name of Magnus (The Great) after his participation in the civil war on Sulla's winning side would, following his victorious campaigns in Asia against Mithridates VI (135–63 BC), implement a patent comparison between Alexander and himself, presenting himself as the new

Alexander. Caesar's *imitatio*, nonetheless, as stated at the beginning, should be considered a *sui generis* kind of emulation: his imitation mainly consisted of comparisons of results, of dreams of conquests and expansion, of the age at which such goals were realized, of their short versus long-lasting quality. Caesar would not clumsily imitate the Macedonian's ways, yet Alexander was certainly a model for him and the idea that some of his acts were inspired or influenced by his desire to be compared with the Macedonian, can be considered within the realm of possibility.

Many neurology textbooks cite Alexander among sufferers of epilepsy and a certain tradition exists that he was epileptic.[25] Unlike Caesar's epilepsy however:

a. compared to his drunkenness, for instance, it has no necessarily central pathological relevance in his life and death, thus it has not been fully investigated;
b. even diagnostic proposals about his death that include it do not absolutely need it to be made, and it is but one of the possible presentations;
c. the evidence in the sources is very scant, much more than for Caesar.

The oldest reference to a potential epileptic-like episode can be mainly found in the accounts by Plutarch and Curtius Rufus. Plutarch describes the episode that occurred in Cilicia, where Alexander suddenly became sick and is cured by a doctor called Philip the Acarnanian, who gives him a remedy, which causes a set of coma-like symptoms, before his health returns.[26] Plutarch gives two possibilities: either Alexander became sick because of fatigue or because he swam in the icy cold waters of the river Cydnus. Curtius Rufus[27] selects this version of the story but does not mention the physician. From this it can be inferred that either the cold-caused trembling/shaking or the initial physical response to the treatment administered by the physician gave the impression of seizures. With this evidence, it is impossible to conclude whether Alexander suffered from epilepsy, whatever the cause. A stronger, albeit purely circumstantial, link to stories of Alexander being epileptic is given by two extra facts:

i.   his brother Philip Arrhidaeus (c. 356 – 317 BC) was mentally retarded and suffered from epilepsy;

ii. through his father Philip, he claimed ancestry from Heracles – who was, as we saw, described as a melancholic epileptic.

In summary, Caesar, who knew Alexander's story perfectly and emulated him, might have been aware of such stories, or rather misunderstandings of history, which might have given birth to one of the several myths about the Macedonian conqueror. If Caesar knew about this as well as the divine connection described earlier and the strong link to Hercules, it cannot be excluded that he counted Alexander in the number of melancholic/epileptic heroes of old and that when passing off his non-epileptic disease as real epilepsy, he had the Macedonian and the Cilician incident in mind. This would have certainly fitted the likely scenario described above, yet, because of the paucity of sources both about Alexander's epilepsy and how the disease was first associated with his name, this digression will, however, remain but a suggestion.

Augustus

Octavian Augustus was the next Roman to have the republic at his feet. After the battle of Actium, nobody was willing to shed more blood and accepted Caesar's adopted son's will as their new code of law. For his part, Octavian respected and restored many of the republican institutions, customs and traditions, giving the impression of being more of a lord protector, a father of the nation, a prince who would still respect the senate and the people of Rome. Of course, this was but an external decoration, since *de facto* his power was supreme and whoever tried to oppose him would be crushed. Under Augustus, Caesar's deification, the process by which his adoptive father came to be counted amongst the gods as *Divus Julius* reached its peak. Caesar the god watched over the destiny and fortune of the Julian house of which Augustus was the leader. His image and memory had to be pure, perfect, and superhuman. Along the lines of what we said about Caesar himself and his reasons, had epilepsy been regarded solely as a curse, what would be the point in making his uncle/adoptive father a most perfect god and the same time leaving such an ignoble mark in historical records? We know that Augustus exerted censorship with great diligence and works by poets of the calibre of Ovid (43–18 BC) and even Julius Caesar's early poetic compositions were suppressed. If he wanted, he could have easily have had references and descriptions of epilepsy removed or softened, so as not to put Caesar's new godly image at stake. Yet he did nothing. This strongly points to his desire to preserve the epileptic tradition since it increased his late uncle/father's divine status. Hercules was thought to have had epilepsy, won immortal glory and ultimately ascended to the world of the gods, winning divine status, just like Caesar. Preserving the epileptic suspicion or even stating it in clear terms, conferred an aura of mystery on the noble founder of the dynasty now destined to rule a new-born empire. As a young man Caesar would likely boast of his descent from Venus at the same time lamenting about the decline of his family. Now he had replaced Venus and Aeneas and the Julian family, restored to its glory, was reigning supreme again.

In sum, we put forward the idea that if the epileptic theory proved very successful, six main reasons may be identified;

1. Caesar's symptoms were visible and could not be denied.
2. They were general and vague and could be interpreted either way, epileptic or non-epileptic.
3. Caesar turned this weakness into a political advantage by playing on people's superstition and the fine line between madness/curse and genius/aura of sacredness.
4. Augustus endorsed this line, although it is impossible to determine whether it was more to his advantage or his uncle's, if this idea became stronger.
5. A final word not having been said on the matter; a tradition of him being epileptic existing, *morbus comitialis* including conditions from utter simulation to *grand mal* epilepsy and a Greek biographer incapable of understanding the subtleties of the Latin language, turning the idea that Caesar was an epileptic into widely accepted fact.
6. Later scholars studying the problem, from Petrarch to modern times, largely accepting the epileptic assumption, directing their efforts to the identification of the cause of this epilepsy, alternatively looking for an

inheritance within the whole family or for diseases occurring to him in later life and causing him to develop late onset epilepsy.

The German philosopher Arthur Schopenhauer (1788–1860) wrote that 'the scenes in our life resemble pictures in a rough mosaic; they are ineffective from close up, and have to be viewed from a distance if they are to seem beautiful'.[28] To understand Caesar's disease and its impact on history, one cannot simply focus on isolated details, one has to contemplate the greater picture of which those are but single elements. To achieve that, one has to take a step back and behold the intricacies and sublime meshwork, in military affairs as well as in pathology, looking for the key to an enigma worthy of the founder of a world empire.

This is what we, to the best of our ability and animated by genuine historical and medical passion, have endeavoured to do in this book.

Notes

Passages quoted from the ancient authors are indicated according to the division of the original text given in the chosen translations.

Preface
1. The opening citation is found in Suetonius and in the original Latin sounds like *'eatur quo deorum ostenta et inimicorum iniquitas vocat. Iacta alea est.'* (*Divus Iulius*, 32).
2. The best sources are undoubtedly Caesar's own commentaries, *De Bello Gallico, De Bello civili* and the three successive anonymous books on the Alexandrian, African and Spanish Wars. Dio Cassius, Appian as well as the cited biographies by Plutarch (The Life of Caesar) and Suetonius' *Vitae Caesarum, Divus Iulius*, furnish excellent accounts of his life. Additional information may be found in contemporary authors such as Cicero (his letters). Were one to prefer modern English-language accounts to primary sources, Adrian Goldsworthy's voluminous tome *Caesar, Life of a Colossus* (Yale University Press, 2006) is certainly a very informative introduction to the topic, while classical publications such as Stefan Weinstock's *Divus Julius* (Oxford, 1971) offer a very solid description of the Roman leader's character and deeds.
3. These are the opening lines of the mock-heroic satire *Mac Flecknoe; or, A satyr upon the True-Blew-Protestant Poet, T.S* by John Dryden *(1631–1700)*, published in 1682.
4. The authors published their preliminary study in the form of a medical hypothesis in the journal *Neurological Sciences* with the title *Has the diagnosis of a stroke been overlooked in the symptoms of Julius Caesar?* (2015 March 29, epub ahead of print).
5. The quotation is taken from the English translation of *The Prince* (1513) edited by Quentin Skinner and Russell Price (Cambridge, 1988). The original Italian reads: *'perchè così come coloro che disegnano i paesi, si pongono bassi nel piano a considerare la natura de' monti e de' luoghi alti, e per considerare quella de' bassi si pongono alti sopra i monti; similmente, a cognoscer bene la natura de' popoli bisogna esser Principe, ed a cognoscer bene quella de' Principi conviene essere popolare.'*
6. The pun nicely fits the turmoil of the last years of the Roman Republic. The misconception, however, that Caesar was born through a caesarean section lasted for a long time and we will discuss this in Chapter One. For more information on the topic, cf Raju, TN. *The birth of Caesar and the caesarean misnomer*. Am J Perinatol. 2007 November 24(10):567–8.

Chapter 1
1. Musgrave J, Prag AJNW, Neave R, Fox RL, White H. The Occupants of Tomb II at Vergina. Why Arrhidaios and Eurydice must be excluded. *Int J Med Sci* 2010; 7(6).

2. Suetonius, *Divus Iulius*, 84.

3. Cf. Borda M, '*Il ritratto tuscolano di Giulio Cesare*,' RendPontAcc 20, 1943–1944 (1945) 347–82 for a detailed description of what is considered the only surviving bust to have been sculpted during his lifetime. It is thus regarded as a prototype for later representations. For pathological interpretations, cf. Chapter Two *sub voce Head Trauma* and Chapter Three. A bust found in the Rhone in 2007 has also been regarded by some scholars as an image of the conqueror made while he was alive, but this interpretations has stirred a heated debate, with prominent views endorsing the thesis that in fact it does not represent Caesar, but some other Roman (in particular Professor Mary Beard's reply, A Don's Life entry 'The face of Julius Caesar? Come off it!' http://timesonline. typepad.com/dons_life/2008/05/the-face-of-jul.html, consulted Jan 06 2016). For suggestions of numismatic evidence of disease, cf. Macchi S, Reggi G *Le condizioni di salute di Cesare nel 44 A.C.* And Chapter Three. Coins are certainly helpful to identify busts and that was likely the case with the Tusculum bust, yet not too much can be inferred from them, or, even if so, it appears not to be supported by the literary sources.

4. Pelling C. (2011) *Plutarch Caesar: Translated with an Introduction and Commentary*. OUP, Oxford, 2007. p. 214.

5. Appian, II, 147.

6. Such scepticism seems to be characterized as more private behaviour which probably only his intimates could witness. He most certainly had had such a mind-set since his boyhood but he soon learned the role of superstition and its use as a weapon to influence the masses. We will discuss this aspect at length in Chapter Five.

7. Dio Cassius, XLVI, 18.

8. Pelling C. (2011) Sources and Method. In Introduction. In *Plutarch Caesar: Translated with an Introduction and Commentary*. Pp. 36–58.

9. Written in the third person and fact-based, no personal reflections, in the style of modern memoirs or diaries, are to be found, in particular, no hints about their composer's weaknesses.

10. Although the debate on his malaria and other alleged diseases in his youth will likely require more Ciceronian argumentations.

11. Cf. Adrian Goldsworthy (2006) *Caesar: Life of a Colossus*, p. 30.

12. Napoleon III. *The History of Julius Caesar*. Vol 1, Chapter 1, note I pp. 295–296. Cf. also Hughes JR. *Dictator Perpetuus: Julius Caesar—did he have seizures? If so, what was the etiology?* Epilepsy Behav. 2004 Oct; 5(5): 765–64.

13. Cf. Chapter Four on life expectancy in ancient Rome and percentages of elderly people.

14. cf. A. Goldsworthy, p.48.

15. Pliny the Elder, *Natural History*, 7.54.

16. Napoleon III, *History of Julius Caesar*, Vol. 1, p. 299.

17. **For the caesarean birth myth** vd. Hughes JR *Dictator Perpetuus: Julius Caesar—did he have seizures/* and also cf. Chapter One note 6. Strangely enough, of the many more likely etymologies, this explanation for Caesar's name has somehow won its place in people's minds. It is not unlikely that for his part Caesar would promote the elephant-deriving variant since the very image can be seen on coins bearing his name. That could have been part of a propaganda strategy: this use of powerful symbols to win

people's attention and deference will become fully self-explanatory in Chapter Five. An ambiguity between caesarean section and elephant can be found in Maurus Servius Honoratus' (fourth and fifth centuries AD) *Commentary on the Aeneid of Virgil* (1.286: […] *Caesar vel quod caeso matris ventre natus est, vel quod avus eius in Africa manu propria occidit elephantem*, '[the name] Caesar because he was born from his mother's cut womb, or because one ancestor of his killed an elephant in Africa by his own hand) and in the *Historia Augusta* (Aelius 2.3). Vd. also Napoleon III, Volume 1, p. 283. **For the Etruscan-derived etymology**, vd. Pelling C. (2011) p. 132.

18. Plutarch, *Caesar*, 1.
19. Suetonius, *Caesar*, 1 – which may also be translated as 'almost every night' – this clearly points to his inability to rest at all since, as if he were but a wild beast, all his energies were used to avoid being caught by Sullan hunters.
20. Majori G. *Short History of Malaria and Its Eradication in Italy with Short Notes on the Fight against the Infection in the Mediterranean Basin. Mediterr J Hematol Infect Dis.* 2012; 4(1): e2012016.
21. Celsus, *De Medicina*, III, 3.
22. Idem, III, 15.
23. Mishra SK, Newton CR. *Diagnosis and management of the neurological complications of falciparum malaria. Nat Rev Neurol.* 2009 Apr; 5(4):189–98.
24. Ridley, R.T. (2000) *'The Dictator's mistake: Caesar's escape from Sulla'*, Historia, 49, pp. 211–29. We thank Dr R Bianucci (University of Turin) for her commentary on this specific work.
25. Plutarch, *Caesar*, 1-2.
26. Montemurro N, Benet A, Lawton MT. *Julius Caesar's Epilepsy: Was It Caused by A Brain Arteriovenous Malformation?* World Neurosurgery. 2015 Dec; 84(6):1985–7.
27. Suetonius, *Divus Iulius*, 45.
28. Plutarch, *Caesar*, 17.
29. Dio Cassius, XLIII, 32.
30. Plutarch, *Caesar*, 53. Cf. also Goldsworthy (p. 466) who describes this as the only episode in which disease might have heavily interfered with Caesar's control of the situation. Generally speaking this is correct, but the later episodes occurred in 45 and 44 BC should also be considered as potentially influenced by disease and causing him not to be totally in control of what was going on.
31. *Bellum Africum*, 82 (1). In this account the dictator is shown to be hesitating (*dubitante Caesare*), when it would be easy for him and his army to win the battle – cf. Frediani A. (2003) *Le Grandi Battaglie di Giulio Cesare*, Rome, p. 236 for more details on the tactical advantage Caesar's army had gained. His intervention is clearly described: *quod postquam Caesar intellexerit incitatis militum animis resisti nullo modo posse […] signo Felicitatis dato […] equo admisso in hostem inter principes ire contendit*, namely Caesar cannot stop his soldiers' ardour to fight and cash in on the occasion to lead the attack advancing with the first line. C. Meyer (original *Caesar*, Berlin, 1982 – consulted Italian edition Garzanti, Milano, 2004, p. 431–432) voices his scepticism and suggests that it may even be that another horseman advanced wearing the commander's (ie Caesar's) cloak. He then hypothesises that this incident might have been kept secret for a long

time and that behind Plutarch's account of the facts may well hide the (oral) testimony of a very good confidant of Caesar's himself.

32. Cf. Benediktson T. *Plutarch on the Epilepsy of Julius Caesar*, Anc W 1994, 159–164.
33. Vd. Canfora L. (2007) *The Life and Times of the People's Dictator*, p. 274.
34. Plutarch, *Cicero*, 39.
35. Cf. note 32.
36. Plutarch, *Caesar*, 58.
37. Idem, ibidem, 60.
38. Vd. 37.
39. Vd. 37.
40. Vd. 37.
41. Vd. 37.
42. Suetonius, *Divus Iulius*, 78.
43. Appian, II, 107.
44. Dio Cassius, XLIV, 8.
45. Nicolaus of Damascus, FGrH F 130 (22).
46. Suetonius, *Divus Iulius*, 78.
47. Idem, ibidem, 79.
48. Plutarch, *Caesar*, 61. Cf. note 104 of chosen English translation about Brutus meaning 'stupid' and inhabitants of Cymé being celebrated for their stupidity.
49. Dio Cassius, XLIV, 9.
50. The Lupercalia were an ancestral festival (February 13–15) serving an apotropaic function. Noble youths and magistrates ran naked through the city.
51. Plutarch, *Antony*, 12.
52. Appian, II, 110.
53. Suetonius, *Divus Iulius*, 86.
54. Idem, Ibidem, 87.
55. Plutarch, *Caesar*, 63.
56. Appian, II, 115.
57. Dio Cassius, XLIV, 17.
58. Barry Strauss. (2015) *The Death of Caesar*, pp. 109–111, integrating and contextualising an excellent analysis of the episode in medical terms by Professor Carl Bazil.
59. Suetonius, *Divus Iulius*, 81.
60. Plutarch, *Caesar*, 64.
61. Appian, II, 116. Cf. also Canfora: 'At length Caesar arrived, in a litter, rather dispirited by the omens', p. 329

Chapter 2

1. Cf. Galassi FM, Gelsi R. *Methodological limitations of an etiological framing of Ariarathes' goitre: response to Tekiner et al.* J Endocrinol Invest 2015 May; 38(5):569.
2. Hughes JR. *Dictator Perpetuus: Julius Caesar—did he have seizures? If so, what was the etiology?* Epilepsy Behav. 2004 Oct; 5(5): 765–64. Esser A. (*Cäsar und die julisch-claudishen Kaiser im biologischarztlichen* Blickfeld, 1958, passim) also supports the idea that epilepsy was endemic in the Julio-Claudian Family. Since Hughes' work is the most

updated study maintaining this stance, we choose to comment on his work, rather than Esser's.

3. Temkin O. (2010) *The Falling Sickness*. Note 126 in Part One. The Latin text may be found at http://www.bibliotecaitaliana.it/indice/visualizza_scheda/bibit000299 (accessed 15/12/2015).

4. Not to be confused with genetic epilepsy.

5. All quotations are from Hughes's work *Dictator Perpetuus: Julius Caesar--did he have seizures?* (2004).

6. For detailed and easily accessible information on SUDEP: http://www.epilepsy.com/learn/impact/mortality/sudep/sudep-faq (accessed 10/12/2015).

7. Thurman DJ, Hesdorffer DC, French JA. *Sudden unexpected death in epilepsy: assessing the public health burden*. *Epilepsia*. 2014 Oct; 55(10):1479-85.

8. Plutarch, *Pompey*, 53.

9. Valerius Maximus, *Dicta et Facta Memorabilia*, IV.6.4 – authors' translation. We thank Marinella De Luca, teacher of Latin, Greek and Classical Civilisation at the Liceo G Cesare-Manara Valgimigli (Rimini, Italy) for helping us with the exact interpretation of this passage and, more generally, for her interest in the proposed theory.

10. Velleius Paterculus, II. 47.

11. Kanngiesser, F. *Notes on the pathography of the Julian Dynasty*. Glasgow. Med. 1912; 77:428–432.

12. Suetonius, *Divus Iulius*, 52.

13. Tacitus, *Dialogus de Oratoribus*, XXVIII. Translation based on Alfred John Church and William Jackson Brodribb's *Dialogue on Orators* (1876), available on Wikisource: https://en.wikisource.org/wiki/Dialogue_on_Orators (accessed 12/12/2015). It is also referred to other notable women, including Caesar's mother Aurelia Cotta.

14. HBO Rome (2005). It would appear that the model for the fictional character was Clodia (1st century BC), the infamous and libidinous lady Catullus calls *Lesbia*. Cf. Monica Silveira Cyrino (ed.) (2008) Rome Season One: History Makes Television, Wiley-Blackwell, p. 139.

15. McCullough C (2013). *Caesar. Head of Zeus*, pp. 123. Passim. McCullough's novels and passion for the ancient world are a monument to polymathic ambitions and the parallel pursuit of both classics and medicine.

16. Kanngiesser F (1912) relying on Heinrich Schaefer's *Monumenta medica; Originalstellen über Medizin aus den alten Klassikern* in *Deutscher Uebersetzung, kulturhistorisches Bild in launiger Darstellung*. Hamburg, Lüdeking, p. 57.

17. Kanngiesser, F (1912).

18. Benediktson T. *Plutarch on the Epilepsy of Julius Caesar*, Anc W 1994, 159–164.

19. Plutarch, *Cato the Younger*, 24.

20. Plutarch, *Brutus*, 5.

21. Weeber K-W. *Vita Quotidiana nell'Antica Roma*. Edizione speciale per 'Il Giornale' Newton & Compton editori srl – original edition *Alltag in Alten Rom. Ein Lexicon*, Zürich 1995. Pp. 31-32.

22. Kanngiesser, F (1912).

23. http://www.forbes.com/sites/kristinakillgrove/2015/05/15/julius-caesars-health-debate-reignited/#2715e4857a0b4e2fe9945b5e (accessed 12/12/2015).
24. Gomez et al. 1995.
25. Gomez at al. 1995.
26. Suetonius, *Divus Iulius*, 51.
27. Idem, ibidem, 45.
28. Bruschi F. *Was Julius Caesar's epilepsy due to neurocysticercosis?* Trends Parasitol 27(9):373–4, 2011.
29. Vd. Borda M. (1943). We'll come back to this in the first section of Chapter Three.
30. Johansen FS. *The Portraits in Marble of Gaius Julius Caesar: A Review, Ancient Portraits in the J. Paul Getty Museum 1* (I 987), pp. 17–40, specifically p. 27.
31. Suetonius, *Divus Iulius*, 52.
32. Catullus, *Carmina*, 93.
33. Idem, ibidem, 29.
34. Idem, ibidem, 57.
35. Jacoby P. *Études sur la selection chez l'homme*. Paris, 1904.
36. Dio Cassius, XLIV, 7.
37. *Ancients Behaving Badly* documentary, 2009.
38. Donnadieu. (1937); authors' translation.
39. Farhi D, Dupin N. *Origins of syphilis and management in the immunocompetent patient: Facts and controversies. Clinics in dermatology* 28 (5): 533–8.
40. Gaul, JS, Grossschmidt, K, Gusenbauer, C, Kanz, F. *A probable case of congenital syphilis from pre-Columbian Austria. Anthropologischer Anzeiger,* Volume 72, Number 4, November 2015, pp. 451–472(22).
41. Penso G. (1989). *La Medicina Romana*. P. 391.
42. Kanngiesser, F (1912).
43. Riesman D, Fitz-Hugh T Jr. *Epilepsia Tarda. Ann Intern Med.* 1927; 1(5):273–282.
44. cf. Penso G. (1989), p. 340, quoting Pliny the Elder (*Natural History*. XX, 65) and p. 346.
45. Hughes JR. *Dictator Perpetuus: Julius Caesar--did he have seizures? If so, what was the etiology? Epilepsy Behav.* 2004 Oct; 5(5): 765-64.
46. Gomez et al. 1995.
47. Montemurro et al. 2015.
48. McLachlan RS. (2010).
49. cf. note 46.
50. Cf. note 48.
51. Vd. Penso G. (1989), pp. 284-285.
52. Bruschi (2011).
53. Bruschi F, Masetti M, Locci MT, Ciranni R, Fornaciari G. *Short report: cysticercosis in an Egyptian mummy of the late Ptolemaic period.* Am J Trop Med Hyg. 2006 Apr; 74(4):598–9.
54. Caesar C J. *De Bello Civili*, III.40.
55. cf. G. Cesare. *De Bello Civili*, Oscar Mondadori, Milano, 2004. Note 140, page 323.
56. Taylor, M.A, Coop, R.L., Wall, RL. (2007) *Veterinary Parasitology* Blackwell Publishing.
57. Gomez et al. 1995.

58. Jones JM. *Great pains: famous people with headaches. Cephalalgia.* 1999 Sep; 19(7):627–30.
59. Penso G. (1989), p. 344.
60. Retief FP, Cilliers JF. *Julius Caesar (100-44 BC)--did he have a brain tumour? S Afr Med J.* 2010 Jan; 100(1):26-8.
61. Dirckx JH (1986).
62. *Who killed Julius Caesar?* (2004). Atlantic Productions (UK). The study was also summarised in Garofano L, Gruppioni G, Vinceti S. *Delitti e Misteri del Passato. Sei casi da RIS dall'agguato a Giulio Cesare all'omicidio di Pier Paolo Pasolini.* Rizzoli 2008, pp. 17–52.
63. Bursztajn H. *Caveat Caesar. Harv Mag* 2003; 106:19.
64. Macchi S, Reggi G. (1986) *Le condizioni di salute di Cesare nel 44 A.C.* Lugano, Gaggini-Bizzozero.

Chapter 3

1. Napoleon III (1865) *History of Julius Caesar*, Vol. 1, p. 288, as the following excerpts.
2. Borda M, *Il ritratto tuscolano di Giulio Cesare RendPontAcc* 20, 1943–1944 (1945) 347–82. Authors' translation.
3. Johansen FS. *The Portraits in Marble of Gaius Julius Caesar: A Review, Ancient Portraits in the J. Paul Getty Museum 1* (I 987), p. 24.
4. cf. chapter 1, note 28.
5. Townend, G. B. C. *Oppius on Julius Caesar, AJPh* 108 (1987) pp.325–42.
6. Plutarch, *Caesar*, 17.
7. Barry Strauss. (2015) *The Death of Caesar*, Chapter 2.
8. Macchi S, Reggi G. (1986). Authors' translation.
9. Beard GM. *Neurasthenia, or nervous exhaustion. The Boston Medical and Surgical Journal* 217–221.
10. Hughes JR. *Emperor Napoleon Bonaparte: did he have seizures? Psychogenic or epileptic or both? Epilepsy Behav.* 2003 Dec; 4(6):793–6.
11. Lombroso G. *Genio e Follia.* First Italian Edition, Milano, Giuseppe Chiusi, 1864.
12. Musumeci E. *Cesare Lombroso e le neuroscienze: un parricidio mancato*, Franco Angeli, Milano, 2012, p. 81, note 151.
13. cf. note 10.
14. Dragotti, G. *Furono epilettici Cesare e Napoleone? Policlinico (sezione pratica)*, 65 (1958): 271–73. Authors' translation.
15. Donnadieu: *La prétendue épilepsie de Jules César. Mém. de la Soc. des Antiquaires de France*, 8e Série, t. X, 1937. Authors' translation as all passages from Donnadieu's article.
16. Jacoby P. *Études sur la selection chez l'homme.* Second Edition. Paris, 1904, p. 10-11.
17. Suetonius, *Divus Iulius*, 57.
18. Cawthorne T. *Julius Caesar and the falling sickness. Laryngoscope* 68(8):1442-50, 1958
19. Shakespeare W. *The Tragedy of Julius Caesar.* (1599)Edited by Arthur D. Innes. Blackie & Son Limited, London and Glasgow, 1908. Online at https://en.wikisource.org/wiki/The_Tragedy_of_Julius_Caesar_(The_Warwick_Shakespeare) (accessed 16/12/2015). Act I, Scene 2.
20. Vd. Chapter 1. Note 38.

21. Hughes JR. *Dictator Perpetuus: Julius Caesar—did he have seizures? If so, what was the etiology? Epilepsy Behav.* 2004 Oct; 5(5): 765-64.
22. Amyot J. *Les vies des hommes illustres grecs et romains.* Several editions from the first in 1559 until 1567.
23. Plutarch, *Alexander*, 42.2. Plutarch. *Plutarch's Lives*. With an English Translation by. Bernadotte Perrin. Cambridge, MA. Harvard University Press. London. William Heinemann Ltd. 1919. 7. Online at: http://www.perseus.tufts.edu/hopper/text?doc⁻Perseuspercent3Atextpercent3A1999.01.0243percent3Achapterpercent3D42percent3Asectionper cent3D2 (accessed 20/12/2015)
24. Paterson J. *Caesar the Man* (chapter 10) in Griffin M. (ed.) *A Companion to Julius Caesar.* John Wiley & Sons (2015).

Chapter 4
1. Cawthorne T. *Julius Caesar and the falling sickness. Laryngoscope* 68(8):1442–50, 1958.
2. cf. chapter 3 note 5.
3. Plutarch, *Demosthenes*, 2.2-3.
4. cf. La Penna A's introductory essay to the Life of Caesar in *Plutarco Alessandro e Cesare*, BUR, Bergamo, 2004 (18th edition), pp. 221–222.
5. Lucretius, *De Rerum Narura*, 3.503 – 508. English translation by William Ellery Leonard. E. P. Dutton. 1916., online at http://www.perseus.tufts.edu/hopper/text?doc=Lucr.per cent203.502&lang=original (Accessed 18/12/2015)
6. Gao L, Meschia JF, Judd SE, Muntner P, McClure LA, Howard VJ, Rhodes JD, Cushman M, Safford MM, Soliman EZ, Kleindorfer DO, Howard G (2012) *What stroke symptoms tell us: association of risk factors and individual stroke symptoms* in the *Reasons for Geographic And Racial Differences in Stroke (REGARDS)* study. J Stroke Cerebrovasc Dis 21:411–416.
7. cf. Altomare *et al.* 2013.
8. Again cf. Suetonius' and Plutarch's general descriptions in chapter 1.
9. cf. chapter 2, note 62.
10. http://elpais.com/elpais/2015/04/10/ciencia/1428658327_819718.html   (accessed 18/12/2015)
11. cf. chapter 2, note 23.
12. Camilo O, Goldstein LB. *Seizures and epilepsy after ischemic stroke. Stroke.* 2004 Jul; 35(7):1769–75.
13. Schulz UGR, Rothwell PM. *Transient ischemic attacks mimicking focal motor seizures. Postgrad Med J* 2002; 78:246–247.
14. Montemurro N, Benet A, Lawton MT. *Julius Caesar's Epilepsy: Was It Caused by A Brain Arteriovenous Malformation? World Neurosurg.* 2015 Dec; 84(6):1985–7.
15. Michelet J. *Histoire Romaine (République).* 7th edition, volume 3. Bruxelles, 1843, p. 194. 'Et jamais César ne fut plus vivant, plus puissant, plus terrible, qu'après que sa vieille dépouille, ce corps flétri et usé, eut été percé de coups.'

Chapter 5

1. Suetonius, *Divus Iulius*, 30.
2. vd. Chapter 2 note 62.
3. cf. the methodological considerations in the opening of Chapter Two. For additional reflections on the role played by pathologies in great men's lives as well as in the creation of mythological figures and the necessity to add their influence to other factors (religious, cultural, anthropological etc.) cf. Armocida E, Böni T; Rühli, FJ; Galassi, FM (2015). *Does acromegaly suffice to explain the origin of Pulcinella? A novel interpretation. European Journal of Internal Medicine.* Eur J Intern Med. 2016 Mar;28:e16-7.
4. Macchi S, Reggi G. (1986) *Le condizioni di salute di Cesare nel 44 A.C.* Lugano, Gaggini-Bizzozero.
5. Galassi FM, Ashrafian H. *Has the diagnosis of a stroke been overlooked in the symptoms of Julius Caesar? Neurol Sci.* 2015 Aug; 36(8):1521-2.
6. Plutarch, *Lysander*, 2. The Parallel Lives by Plutarch, Loeb Classical Library Edition, Vol. 4, 1916. Online at: http://penelope.uchicago.edu/Thayer/E/Roman/Texts/Plutarch/Lives/Lysander*.html (accessed 19/12/2015)
7. Cicero, *Tuscolanae Disputationes*, I.73. Translation from C.D. Yonge *Cicero's Tusculan Disputations*, New York, Harper & Brothers Publishers, 1877.
8. (Pseudo) Aristotle, XXX, 1. Text from *Aristotle. Problems II, Books XXII-XXXVIII with an English Translation by W. S. Hett* London, William Heinemann LTD, Cambridge Massachusetts Harvard University Press, 1958, pp. 155-157. Cf. also the analysis of the question in Paterson J *Caesar the Man* (chapter 10) in Griffin M. (ed.) *A Companion to Julius Caesar.* John Wiley & Sons (2015).
9. Euripides, *Hercules*, 931-934. Translation from *Euripides. The Complete Greek Drama*, edited by Whitney J. Oates and Eugene O'Neill, Jr. in two volumes. 1. *Heracles*, translated by E. P. Coleridge. New York. Random House. 1938. Online at: http://www.perseus.tufts.edu/hopper/text?doc=Eur.per cent20Her.per cent20931&lang=original (accessed 19/12/2015). For the possibility of a partial-complex seizure in this episode, cf. *Deutsches Epilepsiemuseum Kork (Museum für Epilepsie und Epilepsiegeschichte)* website http://www.epilepsiemuseum.de/alt/heraklesen.html (accessed 20/12/2015).
10. Donnadieu: *La prétendue épilepsie de Jules César. Mém. de la Soc. des Antiquaires de France, 8e Série*, t. X, 1937. Authors' translation as all passages from Donnadieu's article.
11. Cf. Canfora L. (2007) *The Life and Times of the People's Dictator*, p. 326.
12. cf. note 10.
13. Temkin O. (2010) *The Falling Sickness.* Note 128 in Part One.
14. cf. Hughes JR. *Dictator Perpetuus: Julius Caesar—did he have seizures? If so, what was the etiology? Epilepsy Behav.* 2004 Oct; 5(5): 765-64. The text (with the authors' translation) is from Hauthal F (ed.) *Acronis et Porphyrionis Commentarii in Q. Horatium Flaccum* (1864), p. 645.
15. Literally the 'downfall' or 'collapse', an expression borrowed from Richard Wagner's (1813–1883) title of the last of the part of *Der Ring des Nibelungen*.
16. Suetonius, *Divus Iulius*, 56.
17. Canfora L. *Quelle poesie e tragedie con troppa politica. E Augusto le censurò. Corriere della Sera*, October 22 2008, p. 41. Online at http://archiviostorico.corriere.it/2008/ottobre/22/Quelle_poesie_tragedie_con_troppa_co_9_081022038.shtml (accessed 20/12/2015).

18. Plutarch, *Caesar*, 11.
19. Suetonius, *Divus Iulius*, 7; Dio Cassius, XXXVII, 52.
20. The episode is also psychologically brilliantly described by Paul Cartledge in his book *Alexander the Great: The Hunt for a New Past*, in the chapter *The Fame of Alexander*.
21. Cf. Canfora L. (2007) *The Life and Times of the People's Dictator*, pp. 17–18.
22. Lucan, 10.13-27. English translation from Pharsalia. M. Annaeus Lucanus. Sir Edward Ridley. London. Longmans, Green, and Co. 1905. Online at: http://www.perscus.tufts. edu/hopper/text?doc=Perseusper cent3Atextper cent3A1999.02.0134per cent3Abook per cent3D10per cent3Acardper cent3D1 (accessed 20/12/2015)
23. *Cleopatra*, film, 1963.
24. Nenci G, *L'imitatio Alexandri*, *Polis*, 4, 1992, pp. 173–186.
25. Cf. Hughes JR. *Alexander of Macedon, the greatest warrior of all times: did he have seizures? Epilepsy Behav.* 2004 Oct; 5(5):765-7.
26. Plutarch, *Alexander*, 19. The authors thank Professor Federico Maria Muccioli for his commentary and views on this passage.
27. Quintus Curtius Rufus, *Historiarum Alexandri Magni Libri Qui Supersunt*, III, 5. '*Vixque ingressi subito horrore artus rigere coeperunt, pallor deinde suffusus est et totum propemodum corpus vitalis calor liquit.*'
28. Schopenhauer A. *Parerga und Paralipomena*, P I I 628. Original quote: '*Der Verlauf und die Begebenheiten unseres individuellen Lebens sind hinsichtlich ihres wahren Sinnes und Zusammenhanges den gröberen Werken in Mosaik zu vergleichen. Solange man dicht vor diesen steht, erkennt man nicht recht die dargestellen Gegenstände und wird weder ihre Bedeutsamkeit noch Schönheit gewahr: erst in einiger Entfernung treten beide hervor.*'

Essential Bibliography

The purpose of this bibliography is to provide the readers with an essential set of tools from which they may also start investigating Caesar's health. We give classical English translations for the ancient authors and we list the most important articles and books discussed in this book. Articles or book not specifically addressing Caesar's life or of general use in this study can be found referenced in the notes.

Ancient Authors

Appian. Loeb Classical Library, 4 volumes, Greek texts with facing English translation by Horace White: Harvard University Press, 1912 and 1913; the Foreign Wars in Vols. I and II, the Civil Wars in Vols. III and IV. Online at: http://penelope.uchicago.edu/Thayer/E/Roman/Texts/Appian/home.html

Caesar. *The Civil Wars*, Loeb Classical Library, 1914. Online at: http://penclope.uchicago.edu/THayer/E/Roman/Texts/Caesar/Civil_Wars/home.html

Catullus. *The Carmina of Gaius Valerius Catullus*. Leonard C. Smithers. London. Smithers. 1894. Online at: http://www.perseus.tufts.edu/hopper/text?doc=Perseusper cent3Atextper cent3A1999.02.0006per cent3Apoemper cent3D1

Dio Cassius. Loeb Classical Library, 9 volumes, Greek texts and facing English translation: Harvard University Press, 1914 thru 1927. Translation by Earnest Cary. Online at: http://penelope.uchicago.edu/Thayer/E/Roman/Texts/Cassius_Dio/home.html

Nicolaus of Damascus, *Life of Augustus*, Translated by Clayton M. Hall (1923). Online at: http://www.csun.edu/~hcfll004/nicolaus.html

Plutarch, *Parallel Lives*. Loeb Classical Library edition (Cambridge, MA and London), translation by Bernadotte Perrin, 1919. Online at:

Life of Caesar http://penelope.uchicago.edu/Thayer/E/Roman/Texts/Plutarch/Lives/Caesar*.html

Life of Brutus http://penelope.uchicago.edu/Thayer/E/Roman/Texts/Plutarch/Lives/Brutus*.html

Life of Antony http://penelope.uchicago.edu/Thayer/E/Roman/Texts/Plutarch/Lives/Antony*.html

Life of Cicero http://penelope.uchicago.edu/Thayer/E/Roman/Texts/Plutarch/Lives/Cicero*.html

Life of Alexander http://penelope.uchicago.edu/Thayer/E/Roman/Texts/Plutarch/Lives/Alexander*/home.html

Life of Cato Minor http://penelope.uchicago.edu/Thayer/E/Roman/Texts/Plutarch/Lives/Cato_Minor*.html

Suetonius, *The Lives of the Twelve Caesars*. Loeb Classical Library Edition, 1913. Online at: http://penelope.uchicago.edu/Thayer/E/Roman/Texts/Suetonius/12Caesars/Julius*. html

Modern Authors

Altomare R, Cacciabaudo F, Damiano G, Palumbo VD, Gioviale MC, Bellavia M, Tomasello G, Lo Monte AI. *The Mediterranean Diet: A History of Health*. Iran J Public Health. 2013; 42(5): 449–457.

Benediktson T. *Plutarch on the Epilepsy of Julius Caesar*, Anc W 1994, 159–164.

Borda M, *II ritratto tuscolano di Giulio Cesare*, RendPontAcc 20, 1943–1944 (1945) 347–82.

Bruschi F. *Was Julius Caesar's epilepsy due to neurocysticercosis?* Trends Parasitol. 27(9):373–4, 2011.

Bursztajn H. *Caveat Caesar*. Harv Mag 2003; 106:19.

Camilo O, Goldstein LB. *Seizures and epilepsy after ischemic stroke*. Stroke. 2004 Jul; 35(7):1769–75.

Canfora L. *The Life and Times of the People's Dictator*. University of California Press, 2007.

Cartledge P. *Alexander the Great: The Hunt for a New Past*. Pan Macmillan, 2011.

Cawthorne T. *Julius Caesar and the falling sickness*. Laryngoscope 68(8):1442–50, 1958.

Dirckx JH. *Julius Caesar and the Julian emperors. A family cluster with Hartnup disease?* Am J Dermatopathol. 1986 Aug; 8(4):351–7.

Dr Donnadieu *La prétendue épilepsie de Jules César. Mém. de la Soc. des Antiquaires de France, 8e Série*, t. X, 1937.

Dragotti, G. *Furono epilettici Cesare e Napoleone?* Policlinico (sezione pratica), 65 (1958): 271–73.

Esser A. *Cäsar und die julisch-claudishen Kaiser im biologischarztlichen Blickfeld*. Leiden: E.J. Brill; 1958. pp. 134–6, 139.

Galassi FM, Ashrafian H. *Has the diagnosis of a stroke been overlooked in the symptoms of Julius Caesar?* Neurol Sci. 2015 Aug; 36(8):1521–2.

Galassi FM, Gelsi R. *Methodological limitations of an etiological framing of Ariarathes' goitre: response to Tekiner et al.* J Endocrinol Invest 2015 May; 38(5):569.

Gao L, Meschia JF, Judd SE, Muntner P, McClure LA, Howard VJ, Rhodes JD, Cushman M, Safford MM, Soliman EZ, Kleindorfer DO, Howard G (2012) *What stroke symptoms tell us: association of risk factors and individual stroke symptoms* in the Reasons for Geographic and Racial Differences in Stroke (REGARDS) study. J Stroke Cerebrovascular Dis 21:411–416.

Garofano L, Gruppioni G, Vinceti S. Delitti e Misteri del Passato. *Sei casi da RIS dall'agguato a Giulio Cesare all'omicidio di Pier Paolo Pasolini*. Rizzoli 2008, pp. 17–52.

Goldsworthy A. *Caesar: Life of a Colossus*. New Haven, CT: Yale University Press, 2006.

Griffin M. *A Companion to Julius Caesar*. John Wiley & Sons, 2015.

Hughes JR. *Emperor Napoleon Bonaparte: did he have seizures? Psychogenic or epileptic or both?* Epilepsy Behav. 2003 Dec; 4(6):793–6.

Hughes JR. *Alexander of Macedon, the greatest warrior of all times: did he have seizures?* Epilepsy Behav. 2004 Oct; 5(5):765–7.

Hughes JR. Dictator Perpetuus. *Julius Caesar–did he have seizures? If so, what was the etiology?* Epilepsy Behav. 2004 Oct; 5(5): 765–64.

Jacoby P. *Études sur la selection chez l'homme.* Second Edition. Paris, 1904.

Jones JM. *Great pains: famous people with headaches.* Cephalalgia. 1999 Sep; 19(7):627–30.

Kanngiesser, F. *Notes on the pathography of the Julian Dynasty.* Glasgow. Med. 1912; 77:428–432.

Macchi S, Reggi G. (1986) *Le condizioni di salute di Cesare nel 44 A.C.* Lugano, Gaggini-Bizzozero.

McLachlan RS. *Julius Caesar's late onset epilepsy: a case of historic proportions.* Can J Neurol Sci 37(5):557–61, 2010.

Michelet J. *Histoire Romaine (République).* 7th edition, volume 3. Bruxelles, 1843.

Montemurro N, Benet A, Lawton MT. *Julius Caesar's Epilepsy: Was It Caused by A Brain Arteriovenous Malformation?* World Neurosurg. 2015 Dec; 84(6):1985–7.

Napoleon III (Emperor of France) *History of Julius Caesar,* 2 Vols. Harper & Brothers, 1865.

Nenci G, *L'imitatio Alexandri,* Polis, 4, 1992, pp. 173–186.

Pelling C. *Plutarch's Caesar: Translated with an Introduction and Commentary.* OUP Oxford, 27-Oct-2011, pp. 519.

Penso G. *La Medicina Romana.* Ciba-Geigy Edizioni. 1989.

Raju TN. *The birth of Caesar and the caesarean misnomer.* Am J Perinatol. 2007 Nov; 24(10):567–8.

Retief FP, Cilliers JF. *Julius Caesar (100–44 BC)–did he have a brain tumour?* S Afr Med J. 2010 Jan; 100(1):26–8.

Ridley RT. *The Dictator's Mistake: Caesar's Escape from Sulla* Historia 49, 2000, pp. 225–226.

Schulz UGR, Rothwell PM. *Transient ischemic attacks mimicking focal motor seizures.* Postgrad Med J 2002; 78:246–247.

Strauss B. *The Death of Caesar: The Story of History's Most Famous Assassination.* Simon and Schuster, 2015.

Temkin O. *The Falling Sickness: A History of Epilepsy from the Greeks to the Beginnings of Modern Neurology.* JHU Press, 29-dic-2010 – pp. 488.

Vinay Kumar, Abul K. Abbas, Jon C. Aster. *Robbins & Cotran Pathologic Basis of Disease.* Elsevier Health Sciences, 2014.

Weber Karl-Wilhelm. *Vita quotidiana nell'antica Roma.* Newton & Compton *editori srl. Edizione Speciale per il Giornale,* 2003.

TV Documentaries

Who killed Julius Caesar? (2004). Atlantic Productions (UK).

Ancients Behaving Badly. Episode 3. (2009) Network: The History Channel.

Index